Level 1 | Part 1

WORKBOOK: HOMEWORK AND CHARACTER BOOK
作业和写字簿
to Accompany

Chinese Link

中 文 天 地
Zhōng   Wén   Tiān   Dì

Elementary Chinese

Simplified Character Version

吴素美　　于月明　　张燕辉　　田维忠
Sue-mei Wu   Yueming Yu   Yanhui Zhang   Weizhong Tian

Carnegie Mellon University

PEARSON Prentice Hall · world Languages

Upper Saddle River, New Jersey 07458

Acquisitions Editor: Rachel McCoy
Publishing Coordinator: Claudia Fernandes
Executive Director of Market Development: Kristine Suárez
Director of Editorial Development: Julia Caballero
Production Supervision: Nancy Stevenson
Project Manager: Margaret Chan, Graphicraft
Assistant Director of Production: Mary Rottino
Supplements Editor: Meriel Martínez Moctezuma
Media Editor: Samantha Alducin
Media Production Manager: Roberto Fernandez
Prepress and Manufacturing Buyer: Christina Helder
Prepress and Manufacturing Assistant Manager: Mary Ann Gloriande
Cover Art Director: Jayne Conte
Marketing Assistant: William J. Bliss
Publisher: Phil Miller
Cover image: Jerry Darvin

This book was set in 12/15 Sabon by Graphicraft Ltd., Hong Kong, and was printed and bound by BRR. The cover was printed by BRR.

© 2007 by Pearson Education, Inc.
Upper Saddle River, NJ 07458

Printed in the United States of America
10 9 8 7 6 5 4 3 2

ISBN 0-13-156441-2

Pearson Education Ltd., *London*
Pearson Education Australia Pty, Limited, *Sydney*
Pearson Education Singapore Pte. Ltd.
Pearson Education North Asia Ltd., *Hong Kong*
Pearson Education Canada, Ltd., *Toronto*
Pearson Educación de México, S.A. de C.V.
Pearson Education – Japan, *Tokyo*
Pearson Education Malaysia Pte. Ltd.
Pearson Education, *Upper Saddle River,* New Jersey

目录　CONTENTS

Character Book Indices

拼音作业一　　Pinyin Homework I

Simple finals: a o e i u ü　　　*Labial initials: b p m f*　　　*Alveolar initials: d t n l*

-1 Listen and circle the right final:

1. lū　lú　lǔ　lù　　　5. dē　dé　dě　dè
2. fū　fú　fǔ　fù　　　6. mō　mó　mǒ　mò
3. pī　pí　pǐ　pì　　　7. tī　tí　tǐ　tì
4. nā　ná　nǎ　nà　　　8. bā　bá　bǎ　bà

-2 Listen and circle the right initial:

1. mù　nù　　　4. lǔ　nǔ　　　7. lǔ　nǔ　　　10. nǐ　lǐ
2. pā　tā　　　5. pà　bà　　　8. bè　tè　　　11. tā　lā
3. mó　fó　　　6. tè　lè　　　9. dí　tí　　　12. pū　mū

-3 Listen and fill in the blanks with the right sound:

1. _____　　6. _____　　11. _____　　16. _____

2. _____　　7. _____　　12. _____　　17. _____

3. _____　　8. _____　　13. _____　　18. _____

4. _____　　9. _____　　14. _____　　19. _____

5. _____　　10. _____　　15. _____　　20. _____

Velar initials: g k h   *Palatal initials: j q x*
Dental sibilant initials: z c s   *Retroflex initials: zh ch sh r*

2-1 Listen and circle the right initial:

1. qì	xì	6. zhè	zè	11. cǐ	sǐ	16. rè	chè
2. xī	sī	7. jī	qī	12. shú	chú	17. cā	zā
3. shī	sī	8. rì	shì	13. hù	rù	18. gé	hé
4. jǐ	xǐ	9. zhà	chà	14. lè	gè	19. cū	sū
5. cè	chè	10. zǔ	sǔ	15. xì	shì	20. gē	kē

2-2 Listen and fill in the blank with the right initial:

1. ____ē	11. ____à	21. ____é
2. ____ī	12. ____ú	22. ____á
3. ____è	13. ____ǐ	23. ____ě
4. ____ī	14. ____è	24. ____ì
5. ____ā	15. ____ì	25. ____ū
6. ____í	16. ____è	26. ____ǎ
7. ____ù	17. ____ù	27. ____ì
8. ____ì	18. ____è	28. ____ǔ
9. ____ū	19. ____ǐ	29. ____é
10. ____ē	20. ____ì	30. ____ù

拼音作业三   Pinyin Homework III

ompound finals: ai ei ao ou ia iao ie iu   ua uo uai ui   üe

-1 Listen and mark the right tones:

1. lao	6. hou	11. kuo	16. nuo
2. cui	7. hua	12. pei	17. hui
3. zhua	8. ai	13. shuo	18. biao
4. liu	9. lüe	14. bie	19. tou
5. ren	10. shuai	15. zhou	20. mao

-2 Listen and circle the right sounds:

1. chóu	zhóu	6. cáo	cái	11. jiǎo	xiǎo	16. bǎo	biǎo
2. chāo	qiāo	7. lái	léi	12. bié	béi	17. shāo	xiāo
3. dōu	duō	8. lín	liú	13. lüè	nüè	18. luó	lóu
4. jué	xué	9. dāo	dōu	14. xuē	xiū	19. guò	gòu
5. huó	hóu	10. diū	duī	15. rào	ròu	20. jiā	jiē

-3 Listen and fill in the blanks with the right finals:

1. b_____	8. l_____	15. zh_____
2. p_____	9. g_____	16. ch_____
3. m_____	10. k_____	17. sh_____
4. f _____	11. h_____	18. r_____
5. d_____	12. j_____	19. z_____
6. t_____	13. q_____	20. c_____
7. n_____	14. x_____	21. s_____

拼音作业四 Pinyin Homework IV

Nasal finals: *an en*   *ian in*   *uan un*
               ang eng ong *iang ing iong* *uang*

4-1 Listen and mark the right tones:

1. jiong	6. lun	11. hen	16. nuan
2. xian	7. rong	12. qiang	17. zhuang
3. hun	8. fen	13. heng	18. zhun
4. an	9. cang	14. liang	19. sun
5. qin	10. mian	15. ling	20. ding

4-2 Listen and circle the right sounds:

1. juān	jūn	6. lín	líng	11. xióng	qióng	16. cóng	chóng
2. zhèn	shèn	7. tūn	tuān	12. zhàn	zhèn	17. zhāng	jiāng
3. qiáng	qióng	8. rēng	zhēng	13. háng	huáng	18. xūn	sūn
4. xiàng	xuàn	9. kàn	kèn	14. huán	huáng	19. gèn	gèng
5. rǎn	zhǎn	10. qǐng	xǐng	15. jūn	qūn	20. nián	lián

4-3 Listen and fill in the blanks with the right finals:

1. b_____	8. l_____	15. zh_____
2. p_____	9. g_____	16. ch_____
3. m_____	10. k_____	17. sh_____
4. f_____	11. h_____	18. r_____
5. d_____	12. j_____	19. z_____
6. t_____	13. q_____	20. c_____
7. n_____	14. x_____	21. s_____

拼音作业五 Pinyin Homework V

Special Pinyin and tonal rules

5-1 Listen and fill in the blanks with the right Pinyin:

1. _____   6. _____   11. _____   16. _____

2. _____   7. _____   12. _____   17. _____

3. _____   8. _____   13. _____   18. _____

4. _____   9. _____   14. _____   19. _____

5. _____   10. _____   15. _____   20. _____

5-2 Mark the tones of "yi" (一) and "bu" (不) in accordance with the "yi-bu" tonal rules:

1. ____wǔ____shí
   一五一十

2. ____xīn____yì
   一心一意

3. ____zhāo____xī
   一朝一夕

4. ____chàng____hè
   一唱一和

5. ____mó____yàng
   一模一样

6. ____wén____wèn
   不闻不问

7. ____míng____bái
   不明不白

8. ____zhé____kòu
   不折不扣

9. ____sān____sì
   不三不四

10. ____bēi____kàng
    不卑不亢

11. ____ sī____gǒu
    一丝不苟

12. ____ chéng____biàn
    一成不变

13. ____wén____zhí
    一文不值

14. ____qiào____tōng
    一窍不通

15. ____chén____rǎn
    一尘不染

Comprehensive Pinyin Review

6-1 Listen and circle the right sounds:

1. dàng	dèng	6. lǚ	liǔ	11. yǔ	yǒu	16. zhàn	jiàn
2. lǔ	nǚ	7. bīn	bīng	12. lián	liáng	17. yuǎn	yǎn
3. wō	ōu	8. niè	lèi	13. xiōng	jiōng	18. jiǎo	xiǎo
4. jié	zéi	9. dōu	tōu	14. kǒu	gǒu	19. xiù	shòu
5. jūn	zhēn	10. zuō	cuō	15. xià	xiào	20. cāi	sāi

6-2 Listen to the following classroom expressions. Then write them in Pinyin:

1. _____

2. _____

3. _____

4. _____

5. _____

6. _____

7. _____

8. _____

9. _____

10. _____

Lesson 1   Hello!

. Listening Exercises

A. Listen and write out the initials for each of the following words:

1. ____ì   2. ____a   3. ____ué____eng

4. ____ǎo____ī   5. ____e   6. ____ú

B. Listen and fill in the blanks with appropriate finals:

1. W____   sh____   x____sh____.

2. T____   b____sh ____   l____sh____ , t____   sh____   x____sh____.

3. N____   y____   b____sh____   x____sh____   m____?

C. Listen to the dialogue and then mark each statement below as True (✓) or False (✗):

MARY： 你好！

JOHN： 你好！

MARY： 我是学生，你也是学生吗？

JOHN： 不，我是老师。

☐ 1. Mary 是学生。   ☐ 3. Mary 不是学生。

☐ 2. John 也是学生。   ☐ 4. John 是老师。

D. Listen to the dialogue again and write it out in Pinyin:

_____

_____

_____

_____

II. Character Exercises

A. Write out the characters for the following Pinyin:

1. tā _____   2. wǒ _____   3. shì _____   4. shī _____

5. nǐ _____   6. xué _____   7. ne _____   8. lǎo _____

9. yě _____   10. sheng _____   11. bú _____   12. hǎo _____

B. Write out the Chinese characters for each of the following words and then show its stroke order:

English	Character	Stroke order
you		
to be		
student		

C. Write the Chinese characters for the following English words:

1. he _____   2. fine _____   3. teacher _____

4. I _____   5. also _____   6. student _____

7. not _____   8. you _____

II. Grammar Exercises

A. Fill in the blanks in the following dialogue with "吗" or "呢":

A: 你好!

B: 你好!

A: 我是学生，你也是学生 _____?

B: 我也是学生。

A: 他 _____? 他也是学生 _____?

B: 不，他是老师。

B. Complete the following sentences with the help of the clues:

1. 你 _____ 。(a greeting)

2. 我 _____ 。(to be a student)

3. 你 _____ 学生吗? (to be also)

4. 他也 _____ 老师。(to be not)

5. 你 _____? (question — how about) 你 _____ 老师吗? (to be not, either)

C. Insert the words in parentheses at the appropriate place(s) in each sentence. Write the sentences in the space provided.

1. 他学生。(是)

   _____

2. 我是学生，你是学生? (也、吗)

   _____

3. 他是老师，他学生。(不、是)

   _____

IV. Comprehensive Exercises

A. Rearrange the following boxes to form a dialogue. Write the number before each sentence to show the correct order:

Correct order

[ ]	1.	**A:** 你好！
[ ]	2.	**B:** 我不是学生，你呢？
[ ]	3.	**A:** 你是学生吗？
[ ]	4.	**B:** 他也是学生吗？
[ ]	5.	**A:** 不是，他是老师。
[ ]	6.	**B:** 你好！
[ ]	7.	**A:** 我是学生。

B. Complete the dialogue with the help of the clues:

A: 你好！

B: _____！

A: 我是学生，_____？

B: 我不是学生，_____ 。

A: 他 _____ 老师吗？

B: 是，_____ 。

Lesson 2   What's Your Surname?

I. Listening Exercises

A. Listen and circle the correct Pinyin in each pair:

1. qǐngwèn
   Yīngwén

2. tóngxué
   tóngshì

3. nǐ jiào shénme
   nǐ xiào shénme

4. míngcí
   míngzi

5. shuí cuò
   shéi shuō

B. Listen to the dialogues and circle the correct answer:

1. The person's family name is

   a. Hú.

   b. Lú.

   c. Wú.

2. a. Wenying is a teacher.

   b. Xiaomei's classmate is a teacher.

   c. Dazhong Li is Wenying's classmate.

3. a. Yu Ying's teacher is Xuewen Wu.

   b. Yu Ying is a teacher.

   c. Yu Ying is the man's name.

II. Character Exercises

A. Write out the radicals in the following groups of characters:

☐	好　她　姓
☐	吗　叫　呢
☐	请　谁

B. Write the traditional form of the following characters:

学 [ ]

谁 [ ]   师 [ ]

吗 [ ]   问 [ ]

C. Translate the following Pinyin sentences into Chinese:

1. Qǐngwèn, nín shì Lǐ lǎoshī ma?

   _____

2. Nǐde tóngxué jiào shénme míngzi?

   _____

III. Grammar Exercises

A. Please use the following clues to make as many sentences as you can. You need to include positive statements, negative statements, and questions. You may use each word as many times as you need:

李， 学文， 叫， 您， 姓， 名字， 中文， 是， 请问， 我
吴， 老师， 她， 于， 的， 小美， 同学， 不， 什么， 吗

_____

_____

_____

_____

_____

B. Ask a question on the underlined part in the following sentences (use the underlined part as the answer to your question):

1. 我姓<u>吴</u>。_____?

2. <u>她</u>叫李小英。_____?

3. 他是<u>我的同学</u>。_____?

4. 我的中文名字是<u>于文汉</u>。_____?

C. Translate the following phrases into Chinese:

1. My teacher's name   _____

2. His classmates   _____

3. Wenzhong Li's student   _____

4. Your Chinese name   _____

5. Her student's Chinese name   _____

IV. Comprehensive Exercises

A. Complete the following dialogue:

A: 你好！请问，_____?

B: 我 _____ 李，_____ 学文。你呢?

A: _____ 叫吴小英。我 _____ 学生。

B: 她是 _____? 她 _____ 学生吗?

A: 不，她是 _____ 。

B: 她是 _____ 中文老师吗?

A: 不，_____ 我的英文老师。

B. You introduced yourself to all the students in the Chinese class today. Write down what you said in class about yourself. You may add whatever information you want to help others know you better (approximately 50 characters).

Lesson 3   Which Country Are You From?

I. Listening Exercises

A. Listen and circle the six words you hear:

1. Fǎguó   2. shòumìng   3. Zhōngwén   4. Měilìjiān

5. bāgè   6. Shuōmíng   7. měiyìjiā   8. chōngwén

9. Yīngwén   10. nǎr

B. Listen and add the correct tone mark(s) to the following Pinyin:

1. cong   2. Hanyu   3. xuexi   4. nar   5. mingtian

6. guojia   7. yuyan   8. xingming   9. jiaoshou   10. shuohua

C. Listen to the dialogue and write it out in Pinyin, paying special attention to the tones:

_____

_____

_____

_____

II. Character Exercises

A. Write out each stroke of the following characters in the appropriate order:

国 _____

美 _____

说 _____

哪 _____

B. Write out as many characters as you can that use the radicals below:

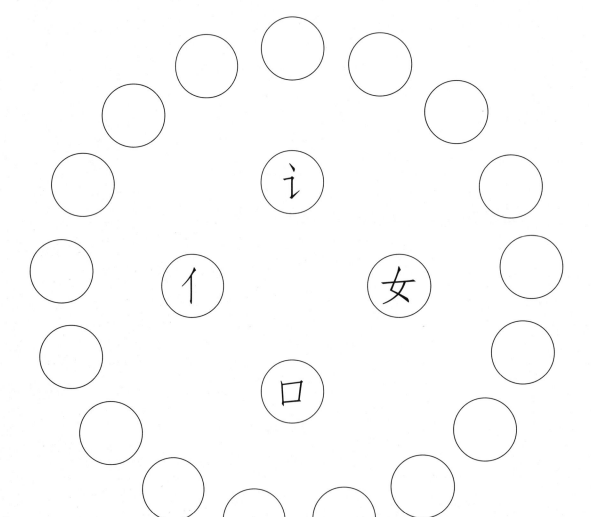

III. Grammar Exercises

A. Complete the following sentences with the help of the clues:

1. 你是 _____ 人？

   我是 _____ 。　　　　　(英国)

2. 我是 _____人 。　　　(中国)

   我说 _____ 。

3. 他是 _____ 。

   他教 _____ 。　　　　(英文)

Note: 教 [jiāo]: to teach

4. 我会 _____ 。　　　　(英)

   我也会 _____ 。　　　(法)

B. Complete the following sentences:

1. 小文是 _____ ，他 _____ 中文 。

2. 李小美 _____ 法国人，她 ____ 说英文，她说 _____ 。

3. 她 ____ 美国人，她说 _____ ，她 ____ 说 _____ 日文 。

Note: 日文 [Rìwén]: Japanese language

IV. Comprehensive Exercises

Someone asks you about your friend who is also in your class. Use the list you compiled in class as a reference to introduce him/her to others. Write as much as you can about your friend (approximately 60 characters).

_____

_____

_____

_____

_____

_____

_____

Lesson 4   What Do You Study?

I. Listening Exercises

A. Listen to the dialogues and fill in the blanks with Pinyin:

1. Zhè shì shénme?

   Zhè shì _____.

   Gōngchéng _____?

   _____.

2. _____ shéi?

   Nà shì _____.

   Tā _____ ma?

   Tā _____.

3. Nǐ xué _____?

   Wǒ xué _____.

   Zhōngwén _____?

   Bú _____, kěshì _____.

II. Character Exercises

A. Write out the Chinese character for each of the following words and then show its stroke order:

English	Character	Stroke order
this		
difficult		
engineering		
homework		

B. Give the radical for the following characters and see whether you can provide more examples of characters with the same radical:

Radical   Examples

1. 课 [ ] _____

2. 你 [ ] _____

3. 吗 [ ] _____

III. Grammar Exercises

A. Ask as many questions as you can on the following sentences:

Example:	这是中文书。 — 这是什么? — 这是什么书?

1. 这是文中的一本工程书。

_____

_____

_____

2. 工程课的功课很多。

_____

_____

_____

3. 英国文学不太难。

_____

_____

_____

4. 中文功课很多,也很难。

_____

_____

_____

IV. Comprehensive Exercises

A. Translate the following sentences into Chinese:

1. Who is he? He is my Chinese literature professor.

   _____

2. What is that? That is an engineering book. That is a book in English.

   _____

3. What do you study? I study French literature. French literature is not very difficult, but there is a lot of homework.

   _____

B. You are going to attend a meeting called by your department. The meeting is to collect your comments on your study and life on campus. The department needs to have some basic information about you before the meeting. Write out a paragraph to introduce yourself (approximately 70 characters).

   _____

   _____

   _____

   _____

   _____

   _____

   _____

Lesson 5　This Is My Friend

I. Listening Exercises

A. Listen to the dialogue and mark each of the following sentences with a "✓" if it is correct, an "✗" if it is wrong:

☐ 1. Xiǎohóng de shìyǒu jiào Měiwén.

☐ 2. Měiwén hé Fāng Míng dōu shì Zhōngguórén.

☐ 3. Fāng Míng jièshào tāde péngyou Xiǎohóng.

☐ 4. Měiwén cháng gēn Xiǎohóng shuō Zhōngwén.

☐ 5. Xiǎohóng yǒu liǎngge Měiguó shìyǒu.

B. Listen to the dialogue and fill in the blanks with correct words or expressions:

吴小英：大文，我来 _____ 一下。_____ 我室友王小红。

李大文：_____ 李大文。你好!

王小红：你好! 你是学生 _____?

李大文：是。我 _____ 工程。你 _____?

王小红：我学 _____。我 ____ 小英 ____ 同学。我们 ____ 学

　　　　　_____ 文学。

II. Character Exercises

A. Pick from this lesson as many characters as you can that start with a horizontal stroke (ˉ):

1. _____   2. _____   3. _____   4. _____   5. _____   6. _____

7. _____

With a vertical stroke (|):

1. _____   2. _____

With a left-slanted stroke (ノ):

1. _____   2. _____   3. _____   4. _____   5. _____   6. _____

7. _____

B. Turn the following Pinyin into characters:

1. liǎngge péngyou _____

2. jǐge shìyǒu _____

3. jièshào yíxià _____

4. cháng shuō Zhōngwén _____

III. Grammar Exercises

A. Fill in the blanks in the following paragraph. Read it carefully and then ask as many questions on the paragraph as you can:

方美文 _____ 中文班的学生。她 _____ 一个室友，_____ 王文英。

王文英 _____ 中国人。她 _____ 一个男朋友，_____ 李中。

李中是美国 _____，他 _____ 学中文。他常 _____ 文英说中文。

他们 _____ 是好朋友。

Note: 班 [bān]: class

_____

_____

_____

_____

_____

_____

IV. Comprehensive Exercises

You share an apartment with your classmates, Wáng Fāng and Lǐ Yīng. You have invited your friend Wú Xiǎowén to come for a party at your apartment. Introduce them and then have a conversation. Write out the conversation using as much from the lesson as you can.

_____

_____

_____

_____

_____

_____

Lesson 6   My Family

I. Listening Exercises

A. Listen, then read the following sentences. Mark "✓" if the statement is correct, and "✗" if it is wrong:

☐ 1. Jiāmíng hé Yǒupéng dōushì cóng Táiwān lái de.

☐ 2. Yǒupéng de bàba bù hěn máng.

☐ 3. Jiāmíng méiyǒu nán péngyou, tā jiějie yǒu.

☐ 4. Yǒupéng de jiā búzài Niǔyuē, zài Bōshìdùn.

☐ 5. Jiāmíng de mèimei méiyǒu māo, yǒu liǎngzhī gǒu.

B. Listen to the paragraph and answer the questions in Pinyin:

1. _____

2. _____

3. _____

4. _____

5. _____

II. Character Exercises

A. Circle the radicals in the following characters:

1. 辆   2. 爸   3. 姐   4. 程

5. 作   6. 狗   7. 没   8. 课

B. Write the following sentences in characters:

1. Wǒ jiā yǒu sìge rén. _____

2. Jiějie yǒu yíge nán péngyou. _____

3. Bàba, māma dōu shì zài Měiguó gōngzuò de. _____

4. Wǒ yǒu liǎngzhī gǒu. _____

5. Wǒ hěn ài wǒde jiā. _____

III. Grammar Exercises

A. Fill in the blank of each phrase with a proper measure word (classifier):

1. 一 _____ 车   2. 一 _____ 狗

3. 两 _____ 学生   4. 三 _____ 书

B. Fill in the blanks in the following paragraph and then ask questions on the highlighted parts:

小美的家_____。他家有_____人：爸爸、妈妈、姐姐和她。爸爸、妈妈都在纽约_____。爸爸有两_____车，_____是日本车。姐姐_____有一辆车，是德国车。姐姐的男朋友_____家文，他是_____来的。

Note: 波士顿 [Bōshìdùn]: Boston

_____

_____

_____

_____

_____

IV. Comprehensive Exercises

A. Translate the following sentences into Chinese:

1. Both Xiaoying and her boyfriend are from China.

   _____

2. My roommate has an American car.

   _____

3. There are four people in my family. We all love our family.

   _____

B. You received an email from 李书文, a student in China who is looking for a pen pal. You have been looking for a Chinese pen pal for a while. Now you want to take this opportunity to make friends with him. Write an introduction about yourself and then ask him some questions to get to know him better.

Note: 笔友 [bǐyǒu]: pen pal

_____

_____

_____

_____

Lesson 7   Where Do You Live?

I. Listening Exercises

A. Listen to the dialogue and circle the right answer:

1. 小美住在哪儿?

   a. 住在宿舍。

   b. 住在校外。

   c. 住在朋友家。

   d. 住在公寓。

2. 小美的房间号码是多少?

   a. 二三五

   b. 五二三

   c. 九二三

   d. 二八五

3. 小美的手机号码是多少?

   a. 三三二 二六八七四六九

   b. 七七二 二二八四七六九

   c. 五三三 六八六二四九七

   d. 八八二 九二八四六七三

4. 小美有几个室友?

   a. 二个

   b. 两个

   c. 三个

   d. 一个

B. Listen to the dialogue and fill in the blanks with the correct Pinyin:

常小西: 书文，你住在那个 _____ 吗?

程书文: 不，我住在 _____，房间号码是 _____。

常小西: 你的 _____ 有 _____ 吗?

程书文: 没有 _____，可是我有 _____。

常小西: 号码是 _____?

程书文: 号码是 _____。

Note: 公寓 [gōngyù]: apartment

II. Character Exercises

A. Comprehensive character exercises:

Process 1: Write down the radical.

Process 2: Count strokes of the character.

Process 3: Write down the correct Pinyin for the character.

Process 4: Make as many words or phrases using the character as you can.

Example: 房 → 户 → 8 → fáng → 房间

	Radical	No. of strokes	Pinyin	Word
1. 间				
2. 号				
3. 校				
4. 机				

B. Write down the traditional form of the framed characters.

1. 哪 | 儿 | _____   2. | 号 | 码 | _____

3. 房 | 间 | _____   4. | 电 | 话 | _____

5. 手 | 机 | _____

III. Grammar Exercises

A. 大王 and 小李 are in the same Chinese class. They often work together in class. Now the professor asks them to find out each other's contact information for future use. Complete the conversation by filling in the blanks with what you have learned in this lesson:

大王：小李，你 ＿＿＿ 在宿舍吗？

小李：对了，我 ＿＿＿ 在学校的 ＿＿＿＿＿＿ 。你 ＿＿＿ 住在学校的宿舍吗？

大王：不，我住在校外，在 ＿＿＿＿＿＿＿＿＿＿＿＿＿＿＿＿＿
(Number 89764 Fifth Ave.)

小李：你的房间 ＿＿＿＿＿＿ 吗？

大王：很大，＿＿＿ 很好。你住在 ＿＿＿＿＿＿＿？

小李：二〇八号。我的房间 ＿＿＿ 不小。你的电话号码 ＿＿＿＿＿＿＿？

大王：＿＿＿＿＿＿＿＿＿＿＿＿＿＿＿＿＿ (103-952-8467)

小李：我的电话号码 ＿＿＿＿＿＿ 六四八二五三一 。

Note: 对了 [duìle]: yes, correct; by the way

Hint: Fifth Ave.: 第五大街 [dì wǔ dàjiē]

B. Translate the following sentences into Chinese:

1. Where do you live?

   _____

2. Do you live on campus?

   _____

3. My brother's dorm is not big.

   _____

4. Your cellular phone number is (142)268-5738, isn't it?

   _____

IV. Comprehensive Exercises

Write a note:

Your close friend is going to visit you over the weekend. Please write a short note providing necessary information such as your address, phone number, and roommates' names, etc.

_____

_____

_____

_____

_____

_____

_____

Lesson 8   Do You Know Him?

. Listening Exercises

A. Listen to the sentences. Translate the question into English and write the answer in Pinyin:

> Example:
>
> Dialogue on the tape:
>
> 韩文英：你认识的中国同学多不多？
>
> 谢国友：很多 。
>
> *Your answers:*
>
> Translated question: *Do you know a lot of Chinese students?*
> Pinyin answer: *Hěnduō.*

1. Translated question: _____

   Pinyin answer: _____

2. Translated question: _____

   Pinyin answer: _____

3. Translated question: _____

   Pinyin answer: _____

4. Translated question: _____

   Pinyin answer: _____

5. Translated question: _____

   Pinyin answer: _____

B. Listen to the dialogue and circle the correct answer:

1. 德朋是从哪儿来的？

    a. 中国   b. 韩国   c. 纽约   d. 日本

2. 文中、德朋和王红今天想去吃什么菜？

    a. 中国菜   b. 韩国菜   c. 泰国菜   d. 日本菜

3. 他们下次想去吃什么菜？

    a. 中国菜   b. 韩国菜   c. 泰国菜   d. 日本菜

II. Character Exercises

A. Write down the traditional forms of the following characters, and then mark their radicals:

Example: 么 | 麼 | | 丿 |

	Traditional form	Radical		Traditional form	Radical		Traditional form	Radical
1. 认			2. 识			3. 课		
4. 后			5. 饭			6. 样		

B. Write the following sentences in characters:

1. Nǐ yǒu shénme shèr ma?

    _____

2. Nǐ xiǎng bù xiǎng huí jiā?

    _____

3. Wǒmen yìqǐ qù Zhōngguó, hǎo bù hǎo?

    _____

4. Xiàkè yǐhòu wǒ xiǎng qù péngyou jiā.

    _____

5. Wǒ bú rènshi nà ge gōngchéngshī.

    _____

III. Grammar Exercises

A. Change the following sentences into interrogative forms by adding the words given in the brackets at the appropriate places:

1. 吴小美是学工程的。   (是吗)

   _____

2. 她今天想回家。   (A 不 A)

   _____

3. 张友朋认识我姐姐。   (对不对)

   _____

4. 他的两个室友都是美国人。   (吗)

   _____

5. 我们下次一起去纽约。   (怎么样)

   _____

6. 下课以后我去吃饭。   (A 不 A)

   _____

B. Translate the following sentences into Chinese:

1. Where are you going?

   _____

2. I have a plan for after class.

   _____

3. Do you want to have dinner with us tonight?

   _____

4. My friend doesn't know our English teacher.

   _____

IV. Comprehensive Exercises

Write a dialogue:

You are going to invite your Chinese friend, 文英, to watch an American movie after class. Please write down the short dialogue between you and 文英. Please use more "A 不 A" questions and tag questions in the dialogue.

_____

_____

_____

_____

_____

_____

Lesson 9   He Is Making a Phone Call

I. Listening Exercises

A. Listen to the dialogue and circle the right answer:

1. 丁明在哪儿?
   a. 在纽约
   b. 在他的房间
   c. 在朋友家
   d. 在宿舍

2. 丁明在做什么?
   a. 在看电视
   b. 在练习中文
   c. 在上课
   d. 在吃日本菜

3. 今天晚上丁明想做什么?
   a. 想看电影
   b. 想去朋友家
   c. 想看小说
   d. 想上网

4. 和丁明打电话的是谁?
   a. 爱文
   b. 小美
   c. 丁明的妹妹
   d. 王红

B. Listen to the telephone messages and mark the correct statements with "✓" and the incorrect ones with "✗":

☐ 1. 电话是小西的同学打来的。

☐ 2. 打电话的人今天晚上想和小西一起去看电影。

☐ 3. 他的电话号码是(一四二)三六六七八九二。

Note: 电影 [diànyǐng]: movie

II. Pinyin and Character Exercises

A. Circle the correct Pinyin to match the words:

1. 正在   zèngzài   zhèngzài   zèngzhài

2. 房间   hángjiān   féngjiàn   fángjiàn

3. 电视   diànsì   diànshì   diánshì

4. 上网   shángwǎng   shàngwǎng   shánghuǎng

5. 时候   shíhou   shéhou   chíhou

6. 今天   zīntiān   jíntian   jīntiān

7. 晚上   wǎngsàng   wánchàng   wǎnshàng

8. 留言   lúyán   niúyán   liúyán

9. 再见   zàijiàn   zhàijiàn   zhuáizhuàn

10. 知道   jīdào   jīdòu   zhīdào

B. Comprehensive character exercises:

Process 1: Write down the radical.

Process 2: Count strokes of the character.

Process 3: Write down the correct Pinyin for the character.

Process 4: Make as many words or phrases using the character as you can.

Example: 话 → 讠 → 8 → huà → 电话

	Radical	No. of strokes	Pinyin	Word
1. 今				
2. 看				
3. 电				
4. 忙				

C. Write down the traditional form of the framed characters:

1. 打 电 话 _____ 2. 看 电 视 _____

3. 上 网 _____ 4. 看 书 _____

5. 对 不 起 _____ 6. 时 候 _____

7. 谢谢 _____ 8. 给 _____

II. Grammar Exercises

A. Complete the sentences with "正在 . . . . . ." and the phrases given:

1. A: 请问小文在吗？

   B: 在，他 _____ 。(看电视)

2. A: 丁老师呢？

   B: 她 _____ 。(休息)

3. A: 姐姐呢？

   B: 她 _____ 。(和男朋友打电话)

4. A: 王红和小美都在学中文吗？

   B: 王红没有在学中文。她 _____ 。(学法文)

B. Translate the following sentences into Chinese:

1. Do you want to leave a message?

_____

2. Please ask him to call me when he is back.

_____

3. May I ask who is speaking, please?

_____

4. He is not watching TV. He is on the Internet.

_____

5. Hold on, please.

_____

IV. Comprehensive Exercises

Leave a message:

You want to go to 小文's dorm to ask him some questions on mathematics this evening, but 小文 is not available when you visit him. Compose a message to leave on his answering machine, telling him about your plan and asking him to call you back when he returns.

_____

_____

_____

_____

_____

Lesson 10   I Get Up at 7:30 Every Day

I. Listening Exercises

A. Listen to 小美's daily schedule of her summer Chinese course in Shanghai, and then mark the correct statements with "✓" and the incorrect ones with "✗":

☐ 1. 小美每天早上八点起床。

☐ 2. 然后九点去学校上课。

☐ 3. 下课以后，小美去图书馆看书。

☐ 4. 下午小美上中文课。

☐ 5. 中文课以后，小美去打球。

B. Listen to 友朋 talk about his daily schedule and write out the time of each activity in Chinese:

1. 起床   2. 睡觉   3. 上课   4. 吃晚饭

_____   _____   _____   _____

5. 去图书馆   6. 打球   7. 学中文   8. 上网

_____   _____   _____   _____

II. Pinyin and Character Exercises

Write out the Pinyin and characters for the following English words or phrases:

	Pinyin	character		Pinyin	character
1. university	_____	_____	2. semester	_____	_____
3. everyday	_____	_____	4. life	_____	_____
5. email	_____	_____	6. library	_____	_____
7. then	_____	_____	8. like	_____	_____
9. write letter	_____	_____	10. play ball	_____	_____
11. get up	_____	_____	12. go to bed	_____	_____

III. Grammar Exercises

A. The following time and activities show what 文英 does every day. Write a paragraph about her daily activities:

10:30 A.M. (use "才")	get up
11:30 A.M. every day	take courses
after class	play ball
4:00 P.M.	study in the library
8:30 P.M.	write emails
12:15 A.M.	sleep

_____

_____

_____

_____

_____

B. Translate the following sentences into Chinese:

1. He went to have Japanese food at 12:30. After that, he went to the library.

   _____

2. I wrote a letter to my elder sister after getting up.

   _____

3. He plays ball at 9:00 P.M. every day.

   _____

4. I like my university life.

   _____

/. Comprehensive Exercises

ort essay:

'rite a letter describing your university life to your parents.

_____

_____

_____

_____

_____

_____

_____

Lesson 11 Do You Want Black Tea or Green Tea?

Listening Exercises

. Listen to the dialogue and mark the correct statements with "✓" and the incorrect ones with "✗":

☐ 1. 小美和于英正在法国饭馆吃饭。

☐ 2. 小美正在喝汤。

☐ 3. 饭馆的牛肉很好吃。

☐ 4. 于英不喜欢喝可乐。

. Listen to the telephone conversation between 方小文 and a waitress in a Chinese restaurant. Check the items and circle the numbers 方小文 has ordered for pick-up.

Note: 拿 [ná]: pick up

方小文点的菜：

☐ 啤酒   1   2   3   4   5

☐ 可乐   1   2   3   4   5

☐ 冰红茶   1   2   3   4   5

☐ 汤   1   2   3   4   5

☐ 炒饭   1   2   3   4   5

☐ 炒面   1   2   3   4   5

 ☐ 饺子   10   20   30   40   50

II. Character Exercises

A. Write the characters for the following words:

1. xǐhuān

2. háishì

3. píjiǔ

4. lǜchá

5. chǎomiàn

6. kělè

7. chǎofàn

8. xiǎng

9. fànguǎn

10. bīnghóngchá

11. xiānsheng

12. xiǎojiě

13. fúwùyuán

14. jiǎozi

15. shuāng

16. pán

3. Write out the radicals for the following characters, count their stroke numbers, and look up their meanings in the dictionary and enter on chart:

Characters	Radical	No. of strokes	Definition
馆	饣	11	house
务			
坐			
员			
喝			
茶			
杯			
红			
冰			
乐			
瓶			
酒			
盘			
面			
筷			

III. Grammar Exercises

A. Ask an alternative question based on the choices given and then answer it:

1. 吃中国菜，吃法国菜

   _____?

   _____

2. 去打球，去图书馆

   _____?

   _____

3. 两点下课，三点下课

   _____?

   _____

4. 是工程师，是老师

   _____?

   _____

5. 有四门课，有五门课

   _____?

   _____

. Fill in the blanks with the proper measure words (some of them may be used more than once):

位　只　个　杯　瓶　辆　盘　碗　双　本

1. 常先生是一 ___ 很好的老师。

2. 我点两 ___ 炒饭和两 ___ 可乐。

3. 爸爸有一 ___ 狗。

4. 我们家有四 ___ 人。

5. 她想喝一 ___ 茶。

6. 我的朋友要一 ___ 啤酒。

7. 那个美国人有一 ___ 车。

8. 那三 ___ 法国人想喝一 ___ 冰红茶和两 ___ 咖啡。

9. 这五 ___ 学生有三 ___ 工程书。

10. 给我们三 ___ 汤和一 ___ 筷子。

. Translate the following sentences into Chinese:

1. Do you like drinking tea or coffee?

_____

2. Which subject do you like to study, literature or engineering?

_____

3. After eating the fried rice, I want to drink a cup of tea.

_____

4. I often go to Chinese restaurants.

_____

IV. Comprehensive Exercises

Three old friends of yours are coming to your apartment for a visit in the evening. But you are unfortunately unable to prepare food for them. You leave a note to your roommate and ask him/her to do you a favor by ordering food from the Chinese restaurant (at least 70 characters). Please include the following words and phrases in the note:

点　要　想　喜欢　杯　瓶　盘　碗　双　谢谢

_____

_____

_____

_____

_____

_____

					kǒu 口				
① 吗 (strokes 1-6)	② 吗	③ 嗎	④ ma: (Part.)　你是学生吗？		⑥ mouth	⑧			
					⑦ 吗 吗				
	⑤ 丶	口	口	叮	吗	吗			

Guide for Students

1) Character with its stroke order indicated by numbers

2) Simplified form of the character

3) Traditional form of the character

4) Pinyin pronunciation, grammatical usage, and example sentence or phrase

5) Stroke order illustrated by writing the character progressively

6) Radical of the character with its Pinyin pronunciation and meaning

7) Ghosted images for students to trace over

8) Dotted graph lines to aid students' practice

Lesson 1   Hello!

13

你	你 你	nǐ: you 你好！	rén 人 (亻) person	亻你 你 你 你 你 亻你 亻你 亻你	
	ノ 亻 亻 亇 伬 你 你			你 你 亻你 亻你 亻你	
好	好 好	hǎo: good 你好！	nǚ 女 female	好 女子 好 好 好 女子 女子 女子	
	く 乡 女 妇 奵 好			女子 女子 女子 好 好 女子	
是	是 是	shì: to be 我是学生。	rì 日 sun	是 是 是 是 是 是 是 是	
	l 冂 口 日 旦 早 早 昰 是			是 是 是	
学	学 學	xué: (学生：student) 学生	子 child	学 学 学 学 学 学 学 学	
	` `` ``` ``` ``` ``` 兴 学 学			学 学 学 学 学	
生	生 生	shēng: (学生：student) 学生	shēng 生 produce	生 生 生 生 生 生 生 生	
	ノ ノ 仁 牛 生 生 生			生 生 生 生 生	

6	吗 吗 吗 嗎	ı 口 口 叮 吗 吗 吗 吗 吗 吗 吗 吗 吗	ma: (Part.) 你是学生吗?	kǒu 口 mouth 吗 吗	吗 吗 吗 吗 吗 吗 吗 吗

| 7 | 我 我 我 | ʻ 一 于 手 扰 我 我 我 我 我 我 | wǒ: I, me 我是学生。 | gē 戈 spear 我 我 我 | 我 我 我 我 |

| 8 | 呢 呢 呢 | ı 口 口 叮 口 听 听 呢 呢 呢 | ne: (Part.) 你呢? | kǒu 口 mouth 呢 呢 | |

| 9 | 也 也 也 | ㄱ 也 也 也 也 也 | yě: also, too 我也是学生。 | yǐ 乙 second 也 也 | |

| 10 | 他 他 他 | ノ 亻 亻 仲 他 他 他 | tā: he, him 他是学生。 | rén 人 (亻) person 他 他 | |

| 11 | 不 不 不 | 一 丆 不 不 不 不 不 | bù: no, not 不是 | yī 一 one 不 不 | |

| 老 | 老 老 | lǎo: (老师: teacher) 老师 | lǎo 耂 old | | | | | |
| | 一 十 土 耂 耂 老 | | 老 老 | | | | | |

| 师 | 师 師 | shī: (老师: teacher) 老师 | jīn 巾 napkin | | | | | |
| | 丨 刂 刂 刂 刂 师 | | 师 师 师 | 师 师 师 师 师 师 | | | | |

第一课 ▪ 你好!

第一课 ▪ 你好! Lesson 1 ▪ *Hello!*

Lesson 2   What's Your Surname?

IS

| 您 | 您 | 您 | nín:
(for politeness)
you
您好 | xīn 心 (忄)
heart | 您 您
您 您 您 |
| ノ | イ | 亻 | 化 | 价 | 你 | 你 | 你 | 您 | 您 | 您 |

| 贵 | 贵 | 贵 | guì: noble,
honored; expensive
您贵姓? | bèi 貝
shell | 贵 贵 |
| 丶 | 丷 | 口 | 中 | 虫 | 虫 | 卦 | 贵 | 贵 | 贵 贵 |

| 姓 | 姓 | 姓 | xìng: family name
我姓李。 | nǔ 女
female | 姓 姓 |
| ㄑ | ㄅ | 女 | 女 | 妙 | 妒 | 姓 | 姓 |

| 请 | 请 | 請 | qǐng: please
(请问: May I ask...)
请问 | yán 言 (讠)
word | 请 请 |
| 丶 | 讠 | 讠 | 讠 | 请 | 请 | 请 | 请 | 请 | 请 |

| 问 | 问 | 問 | wèn: ask
(请问: May I ask...)
请问 | mén 門 (门)
door | 问 问 |
| 丶 | 门 | 门 | 问 | 问 | 问 |

19	的	的 的	de: (Part.) 我的名字	bái 白 white	的 的		
		` ⺅ 卢 白 白 的 的					

20	英	英 英	Yīng: English 英文	cǎo 艹 (⺿) grass	英 英		
		一 十 艹 艹 芇 苹 苹 英					

21	文	文 文	wén: language, writing 中文	wén 文 literature	文 文		
		、 一 亠 文					

22	名	名 名	míng: name 名字	kǒu 口 mouth	名 名 名	名 名	名
		ノ ク タ タ 名 名 名	名 名 名 名 名				

23	字	字 字	zì: character, word (名字 míngzi: name) 名字	zǐ 子 child	字 字		
		、 ハ 宀 宀 宁 字					

24	中	中 中	zhōng: (中文: Chinese; 中国: China) 中文 中国	gǔn ∣ down stroke	中 中		
		、 ∣ 口 口 中					

				kǒu 口 mouth			
叫	叫 叫		jiào: to call 我叫小美。	叫 叫			
	丶 口 口 叫 叫						

				rén 人 (亻) person			
什	什 什		shén: (什么: what) 什么	什 什			
	丿 亻 仁 什						

				piě 丿 left slanted stroke			
么	么 麼		me: (什么: what) 什么	么 么			
	丿 么 么						

				nǔ 女 female			
她	她 她		tā: she, her 她呢?	她 她			
	乚 女 女 如 奴 她						

				yán 言 (讠) word			
谁	谁 誰		shéi: who, whom 她是谁?	谁 谁			
	丶 讠 计 讨 讨 讨 诈 诈 谁 谁						

				kǒu 口 mouth			
同	同 同		tóng: same, similar (同学: classmate) 同学	同 同			
	丨 冂 冂 同 同 同						

第二课 ■ 您贵姓？

Lesson 3   Which Country Are You From?

13

| 哪 | 哪 哪 | nǎ: which
哪国人 | kǒu 口
mouth | 哪 哪 | | | |
| ㇒ 丨 口 叮 吁 吁 呀 哪 哪 | | | | | | | |

| 国 | 国 國 | guó: country
美国 | wéi 口
enclosure | 国 国 | | | |
| 丨 冂 冂 冈 冈 国 国 国 | | | | | | | |

| 人 | 人 人 | rén: person
中国人 | rén 人 (亻)
person | 人 人 | | | |
| ノ 人 | | | | | | | |

| 很 | 很 很 | hěn: very
很好 | chì 彳
step | 很 很 | | | |
| ノ ノ 彳 彳 彳 彳 彳 很 很 | | | | | | | |

| 对 | 对 對 | duì: correct
对了。 | cùn 寸
inch | 对 对 | | | |
| フ 又 又一 对 对 | | | | | | | |

				le: (Part.) 对了。	yǐ 乙 second				
36	了	了	了		了 了				
		⁻ 了							
37	法	法	法	fǎ: France 法国	shuǐ 水(氵) water				
					法 法				
		` ` 氵 氵 汁 泮 法 法							
38	美	美	美	měi: USA 美国	yáng 羊 sheep				
					美 美				
		` ` 丷 丷 羊 羊 羊 美 美							
39	说	说	說	shuō: speak 说中文	yán 言(讠) word				
					说 说				
		` 讠 讠 讠 说 说 说 说 说							
40	会	会	會	huì: can 会说中文	rén 人(亻) person				
					会 会				
		丿 人 仝 仝 会 会							
41	一	一	一	yī: one 一点儿	yī 一 one				
					一 一				
		一							

点	点	點	diǎn: dot 一点儿	huǒ 火 (灬) fire			
				点 点			
丨	卜	卜	占	占	占	点	点

儿	儿	兒	ér: (retroflex ending) (一点儿: a little bit) 一点儿	ér 儿 walking man			
				儿 儿			
丿	儿						

和	和	和	hé: and 我和你	kǒu 口 mouth			
				和 和			
一	二	千	禾	禾	和	和 和	和 和

程程

Name: _____ Date: _____

13

	那	那	nà: that 那是	yì 邑 (阝) city			
	丁	⁊	ⱻ	月	那	那		那 那			

	书	書	shū: book 英文书	gǔn 丨 down stroke			
	⁊	⁊	书	书				书 书			

	这	這	zhè: this 这是	chuò 辵 (辶) motion			
	⟍	二	亇	文	文	议	这	这 这			

	本	本	běn: (M.W.) 一本书	mù 木 wood			
	一	十	才	木	本			本 本			

	工	工	gōng: work (工程: engineering) 工程	gōng 工 work			
	一	丁	工					工 工			

				chéng: (工程: engineering) 工程	hé 禾 grain	程 程		
50	程	程	程			程 程		
		丿	二	千	千	禾	禾	秆	秆	秆	秆	程	程

				nán: difficult 不难	zhuī 隹 short-tailed birds		
51	难	难	難			难 难	
		丁	又	对	对	对	难	难	难	难

				tài: too 太难	dà 大 big		
52	太	太	太			太 太	
		一	大	大	太

				kě: but (可是: but) 可是	kǒu 口 mouth		
53	可	可	可			可 可	
		一	一	丆	口	可

				gōng: (功课: homework; assignment) 功课	gōng 工 work		
54	功	功	功			功 功	
		一	丁	工	功	功

				kè: class (功课: homework; assignment) 功课	yán 言 (讠) word		
55	课	课	課			课 课	
		丶	讠	讠	沪	淈	诨	诨	课	课	课

多	多	多	duō: many, much 很多	xī 夕 night			
	ノ	ク	夕	多	多	多	
				多	多		

| 们 | 们 | 們 | men: (used after a personal pronoun or a noun to show plural number); (他们: they) 我们 | rén 人 (亻) person | | | |
| | ノ | 亻 | 亻 | 价 | 们 | 们 | 们 |

| 少 | 少 | 少 | shǎo: few, little 不少 | xiǎo 小 small | | | |
| | 丨 | 小 | 小 | 少 | 少 | 少 | |

Lesson 5   This Is My Friend

13

朋	朋 朋	péng: friend (朋友: friend) 朋友	ròu 肉 (月) meat 朋 朋		
	ノ 刀 月 月 刖 朋 朋 朋				

友	友 友	yǒu: friend (朋友 péngyou: friend) 朋友	yòu 又 right hand 友 友		
	一 ナ 方 友				

来	来 来	lái: come 我来介绍一下。	yī 一 one 来 来		
	一 ㇐ 冂 立 平 来 来				

介	介 介	jiè: (介绍: introduce) 介绍	rén 人 (亻) person 介 介		
	ノ 人 介 介				

绍	绍 绍	shào: (介绍: introduce) 介绍	mì 糸 (纟) silk 绍 绍		
	ㄥ 纟 纟 纩 纫 纫 绍 绍				

| 64 | 下 | 下 | 下 | xià: down; get off (一下: a little) 一下 | yī 一 one 下 下 | | | | |
| | | 一 丁 下 | | | | | | | |

| 65 | 室 | 室 | 室 | shì: room 室友 | mián 宀 roof 室 室 | | | | |
| | | 丶 宀 宀 宁 它 空 宏 宁 室 | | | | | | | |

| 66 | 有 | 有 | 有 | yǒu: have 我有 | ròu 肉(月) meat 有 有 | | | | |
| | | 一 ナ 才 冇 冇 有 | | | | | | | |

| 67 | 几 | 几 | 幾 | jǐ: how many 几个 | jǐ 几 some 几 几 | | | | |
| | | ノ 几 | | | | | | | |

| 68 | 两 | 两 | 兩 | liǎng: two 两个 | yī 一 one 两 两 | | | | |
| | | 一 ㄧ 厅 丙 两 两 | | | | | | | |

| 69 | 个 | 个 | 個 | gè: (M.W.) 一个 | rén 人(亻) person 个 个 | | | | |
| | | ノ 人 个 | | | | | | | |

| 都 | 都 | 都 | **dōu: all; both**
都是 | yì 邑 (阝)
city | | | |
| 一 | 十 | 土 | 耂 | 耂 | 者 | 者 | 者 | 者阝 | 都 |

| 常 | 常 | 常 | **cháng: often**
常说中文 | jīn 巾
napkin | | | |
| 丨 | 丬 | 丬 | 兴 | 兴 | 兴 | 常 | 常 | 常 | 常 | 常 |

| 跟 | 跟 | 跟 | **gēn: with**
跟他 | zú 足
foot | | | |
| 口 | 口 | 口 | 足 | 足 | 趴 | 趴 | 跟 | 跟 | 跟 | 跟 |

第五课 ■ 这是我朋友　**Lesson 5** ■ *This Is My Friend*

Lesson 6   My Family

/6

家	家	家	jiā: home (大家: all; everybody) 我的家	mián 宀 roof	家	家		
	丶	丶 宀 宀 宀 宁 宇 宇 家 家 家			家	家	家 家	

大	大	大	dà: big (大家: all; everybody) 大家	dà 大 big	大	大		
	一 ナ 大							

从	从	從	cóng: from 从中国来	rén 人 (亻) person	从	从		
	丿 人 从 从							

在	在	在	zài: at; in 在美国	tǔ 土 earth	在	在		
	一 ナ 才 在 在 在							

四	四	四	sì: four 四个	wéi 口 enclosure	四	四		
	丨 冂 冈 四 四							

78	爸	爸 爸	**bà: dad** 爸爸	**fù 父** father 爸 爸	
		ノ 八 ⺈ 父 爷 爷 爸 爸			

79	妈	妈 媽	**mā: mom** 妈妈	**nǚ 女** female 妈 妈	
		ㄑ ㄥ 女 女 妈 妈			

80	姐	姐 姐	**jiě: older sister** 姐姐	**nǚ 女** female 姐 姐	
		ㄑ ㄥ 女 女 如 如 姐 姐			

81	作	作 作	**zuò: (工作: work)** 工作	**rén 人 (亻)** person 作 作	
		ノ 亻 亻 亻 作 作 作			

82	男	男 男	**nán: male** 男朋友	**tián 田** land 男 男	
		㇀ 冂 日 用 田 罗 男			

83	没	没 没	**méi:** (没有: don't have, doesn't have) 没有	**shuǐ 水 (氵)** water 没 没	
		丶 丶 氵 氵 沪 汐 没			

辆	辆 辆	**liàng:** (measure word for vehicles) 两辆车	**chē** 车 (车) vehicle 辆 辆			
一	𠂉	𠂉	车	轩	轩	斩 辆 辆 辆 辆

车	车 車	**chē:** car 美国车	**chē** 车 (车) vehicle 车 车			
一	𠂉	𠂉	车			

只	只 隻	**zhī:** (M.W.) 一只狗	**kǒu** 口 mouth 只 只			
㇆	丨 口	口	尸	只		

狗	狗 狗	**gǒu:** dog 一只狗	**quǎn** 犬 (犭) dog 狗 狗			
丿	犭	犭	犭	狗 狗 狗 狗		

爱	爱 愛	**ài:** love 我爱我的家。	**zhǎo** 爪 (爫) claw 爱 爱			
丿	𠂉	爫	爫	严 严 罗 爱 爱		

Name: _____ Date: _____

Lesson 7   Where Do You Live?

住	住 住	zhù: live 住在	rén 人 (亻) person				
	ノ 亻 亻 仁 仁 住		住 住				

宿	宿 宿	sù: put up for the night (宿舍: dorm) 宿舍	mián 宀 roof				
	丶 丶 宀 宀 宀 宁 宿 宿 宿		宿 宿				

舍	舍 舍	shè: house (宿舍: dorm) 宿舍	rén 人 (亻) person				
	ノ 人 △ 今 全 舎 舍 舍		舍 舍				

号	号 號	hào: number 号码	kǒu 口 mouth				
	丶 口 口 吕 号		号 号				

房	房 房	fáng: house 房间	hù 户 door				
	丶 丶 ユ 户 户 庐 庐 房		房 房				

94	间	间 間	jiān: room 房间	mén 門 (门) door				
				间 间				
		` 丶 门 门 闩 闩 间						

95	电	电 電	diàn: electricity 电话	tián 田 land				
				电 电				
		` 丨 冂 日 旦 电						

96	话	话 話	huà: word (电话: phone) 电话	yán 言 (讠) word				
				话 话				
		` 丶 讠 讠 讠 记 话 话						

97	小	小 小	xiǎo: small 很小	xiǎo 小 small				
				小 小				
		亅 小 小						

98	码	码 碼	mǎ: (号码: number) 号码	shí 石 stone				
				码 码				
		一 丆 石 石 石 码 码						

99	二	二 二	èr: two	yī 一 one				
				二 二				
		一 二						

三	三	三	sān: three	yī 一 one				
	一	二	三		三 三			

五	五	五	wǔ: five	yī 一 one				
	一	丁	开	五	五 五			

六	六	六	liù: six	tóu 亠 cover				
	丶	亠	六	六	六 六			

七	七	七	qī: seven	yī 一 one				
	一	七			七 七			

八	八	八	bā: eight	bā 八 eight				
	丿	八			八 八			

九	九	九	jiǔ: nine	yǐ 乙 second				
	丿	九			九 九			

| 106 | 手 | 手 手 | shǒu: hand 手机 | shǒu 手(扌) hand 手 手 | | | | |
| | | 一 二 三 手 | | | | | | |

| 107 | 机 | 机 機 | jī: machine (手机: cell phone) 手机 | mù 木 wood 机 机 | | | | |
| | | 一 十 オ 木 机 机 | | | | | | |

| 108 | 校 | 校 校 | xiào: school 校外 | mù 木 wood 校 校 | | | | |
| | | 一 十 オ 木 木 村 杧 杧 校 校 | | | | | | |

| 109 | 外 | 外 外 | wài: outside 校外 | xī 夕 night 外 外 外 外 | | | | |
| | | ノ ク 夕 列 外 | | | | | | |

Lesson 8   Do You Know Him?

24

认	认 認	rèn: (认识 rènshi: know, recognize) 认识	yán 言(讠) word	认 认
	` 讠 认 认			
识	识 識	shí: (认识 rènshi: know, recognize) 认识	yán 言(讠) word	识 识
	` 讠 讥 识 识 识			
去	去 去	qù: go 去哪儿	sī 厶 private; cocoon	去 去
	一 十 土 去 去			
上	上 上	shàng: get on, go to (上课: attend class) 上课	yī 一 one	上 上
	⏐ 卜 上			
以	以 以	yǐ: (以后: after, later) 以后	rén 人(亻) person	以 以
	⁄ 𝘭 以 以			

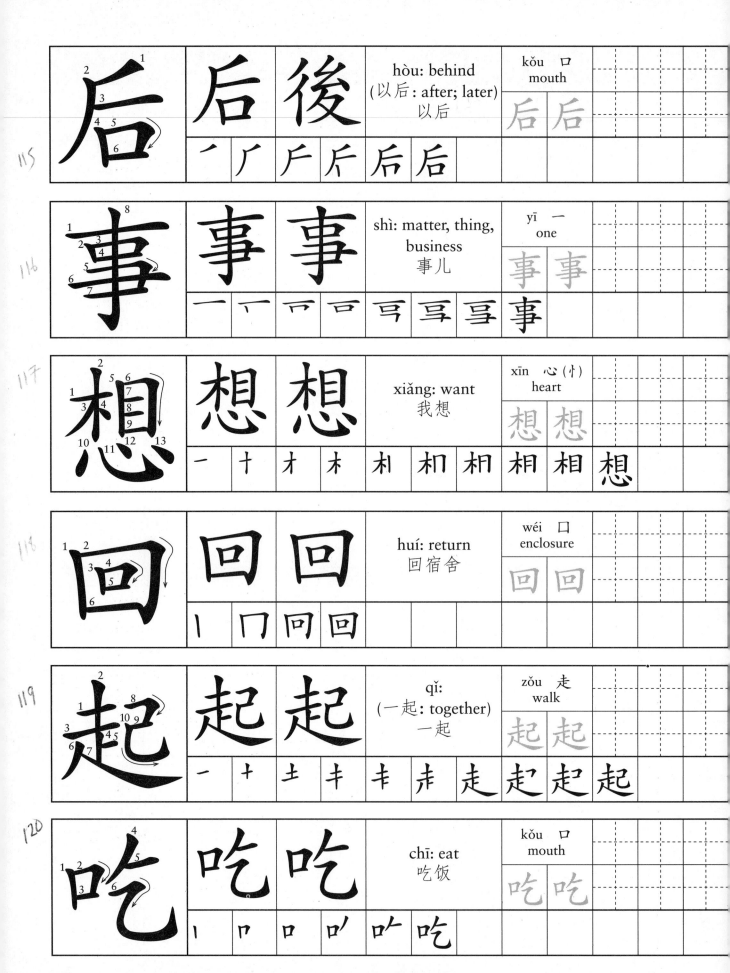

| | 后 | 後 | hòu: behind
(以后: after; later)
以后 | kǒu 口
mouth | | |
| 115 | 一 厂 厂 斤 后 后 | | | 后 后 | | |

| | 事 | 事 | shì: matter, thing,
business
事儿 | yī 一
one | | |
| 116 | 一 一 一 一 弓 弓 弓 事 | | | 事 事 | | |

| | 想 | 想 | xiǎng: want
我想 | xīn 心 (忄)
heart | | |
| 117 | 一 十 才 木 木 和 相 相 相 想 | | | 想 想 | | |

| | 回 | 回 | huí: return
回宿舍 | wéi 囗
enclosure | | |
| 118 | 丨 冂 回 回 | | | 回 回 | | |

| | 起 | 起 | qǐ:
(一起: together)
一起 | zǒu 走
walk | | |
| 119 | 一 十 土 丰 丰 走 走 起 起 起 | | | 起 起 | | |

| | 吃 | 吃 | chī: eat
吃饭 | kǒu 口
mouth | | |
| 120 | 丨 口 口 吖 吃 吃 | | | 吃 吃 | | |

| 饭 | 饭 饭 | | fàn: meal
吃饭 | shí 食 (饣)
food | | | |
| | ノ 𠂉 𫗦 饣 饣 饭 饭 | | | | 饭 饭 | | |

| 菜 | 菜 菜 | | cài: dish
日本菜 | cǎo 艸 (艹)
grass | | | |
| | 一 艹 艹 艹 艹 芏 芏 苹 茓 菜 | | | | 菜 菜 | | |

| 今 | 今 今 | | jīn: (今天: today)
今天 | rén 人 (亻)
person | | | |
| | ノ 人 人 今 | | | | 今 今 | | |

| 天 | 天 天 | | tiān: day
今天 | yī 一
one | | | |
| | 一 二 干 天 | | | | 天 天 | | |

| 次 | 次 次 | | cì: order, sequence
(下次: next time)
下次 | qiàn 欠
owe | | | |
| | 丶 冫 冫 汃 次 次 | | | | 次 次 | | |

| 怎 | 怎 怎 | | zěn:
(怎么样: how)
怎么样 | xīn 心 (忄)
heart | 怎 | | |
| | ノ 𠂉 仁 乍 乍 乍 怎 怎 怎 | | | | 怎 怎 | | |

127	样	样	様	yàng: appearance; sample (怎么样: how) 怎么样	mù 木 wood 样 样	
	一	十	才	木	术	栏 栏 栏 样

128	行	行	行	xíng: okay	chì 彳 step 行 行	
	丿	⺅	彳	彳	行 行	

129	再	再	再	zài: again (再见: see you, goodbye) 再见	jiōng 冂 borders 再 再	
	一	厂	冂	冄	再 再	

130	见	见	見	jiàn: see (再见: see you, goodbye) 再见	jiàn 見 (见) see 见 见	
	丨	冂	贝	见		

Lesson 9　He Is Making a Phone Call

22

			dǎ: hit; play (打电话: make a phone call) 打电话	shǒu 手 (扌) hand			
打	打	打		打 打			
	一	丁	扌	扌	打		

			wèi (wéi): hello, hey	kǒu 口 mouth			
喂	喂	喂		喂 喂			
口	叮	叮	叩	喟	喟	唱	喂 喂 喂

			děng: wait 等一下儿	zhú 竹 (⺮) bamboo			
等	等	等		等 等			
ノ	⺧	⺮	竹	竹	竹	竺	竿 笙 笙 等 等

			zhī: know 知道	shǐ 矢 arrow			
知	知	知		知 知			
ノ	㇒	느	午	矢	知		

			dào: road; talk (知道: know) 知道	chuò 辵 (辶) motion			
道	道	道		道 道			
丶	丷	丷	丷	产	岸	首	首 首 道

136	谢	谢	謝	xiè: thanks 谢谢	yán 言(讠) word 谢 谢			
		`	讠	讠	讠	讠	讠	讠	讠	讠	谢	谢
137	吧	吧	吧	ba: (Part.) 你是小美吧？	kǒu 口 mouth 吧 吧			
		口	口	吵	吧	吧			
138	忙	忙	忙	máng: busy 很忙	xīn 心(忄) heart 忙 忙			
		`	忄	忄	忄	忙	忙		
139	正	正	正	zhèng: in process of 正在	zhǐ 止 stop 正 正			
		一	丁	下	正	正			
140	看	看	看	kàn: see, watch 看电视	mù 目 eye 看 看			
		一	二	三	手	看			
141	视	视	視	shì: look at (电视: TV) 电视	jiàn 見(见) see 视 视			
		`	冫	礻	礻	礻	初	初	视

做	做 做	zuò: do 做什么	rén 人(亻) person				
	ノ 亻 亻 什 估 估 估 做 做		做 做				

网	网 網	wǎng: net 上网	jiōng 冂 borders				
	丨 冂 冈 网 网		网 网				

就	就 就	jiù: (我就是: this is he/she speaking) 我就是	tóu 亠 cover	就			
	、 二 古 方 京 京 京 就 就 就		就 就				

位	位 位	wèi: (measure word for people, polite form) 哪位	rén 人(亻) person				
	亻 亻 什 仁 位		位 位				

留	留 留	liú: leave; remain (留言: leave message) 留言	tián 田 land				
	ノ 𠂊 𠂉 幻 幻 幻 留 留 留 留		留 留				

言	言 言	yán: speech, words 留言	yán 言(讠) word				
	、 二 二 言 言 言 言		言 言				

148	时	时	時	shí: time 时候	rì 日 sun			
					时 时			
	丨	刀	月	日	日一 时 时			

149	候	候	候	hòu: time (时候 shíhou: time) 时候	rén 人（亻） person			
					候 候			
	亻	亻	伫	伫	佢 伫 佢 候 候			

150	晚	晚	晚	wǎn: night 晚上	rì 日 sun			
					晚 晚			
	日	日'	旷	昁	昁 晗 晚			

151	要	要	要	yào: want, desire 要不要	yà 西（覀） cover			
					要 要			
	一	丆	币	襾	西 覀 要 要			

152	给	给	給	gěi: give; for, to 给我	mì 糸（纟） silk			
					给 给			
	ㄥ	纟	纟	纟	纱 纠 纶 给 给			

Lesson 10　I Get Up at 7:30 Every Day

29

			huó: live (生活: life) 生活	shuǐ 水 (氵) water				
活	活	活		活 活				
氵	氵	汗	汗	活				

			qī: a period of time (学期: semester) 学期	ròu 肉 (月) meat				
期	期	期		期 期				
一	十	卄	艹	甘	其	其	其	期

			mén: (M.W.) 五门课	mén 门 (门) door				
门	门	門		门 门				
丶	门	门		乛				

			měi: every, each 每天	mǔ 母 mother				
每	每	每		每 每				
丿	𠂉	仁	勾	每	每	每		

			chuáng: bed 起床	yǎn 广 shelter				
床	床	床		床 床				
丶	一	广	广	庄	床	床		

158	睡	睡 睡	shuì: (V.) sleep 睡觉	mù 目 eye 睡 睡				
		目 目 目 目 目 目 目 睡 睡						

159	觉	觉 覺	jiào: (N.) sleep 睡觉	jiàn 见 (見) see 觉 觉				
		丶 丷 ⺍ ⺍ 兴 兴 兴 觉 觉						

160	半	半 半	bàn: half 十二点半	zhǔ 丶 segmentation symbol 半 半				
		丶 丷 丷 兰 半						

161	才	才 才	cái: (used before a verb to indicate that sth. is rather late) 我十二点半才睡觉。	yī 一 one 才 才				
		一 丁 才						

162	刻	刻 刻	kè: a quarter (of an hour) 九点一刻	dāo 刀 (刂) knife 刻 刻				
		丶 亠 亠 亥 亥 亥 刻 刻						

163	分	分 分	fēn: minute 十点二十分	dāo 刀 (刂) knife 分 分				
		丿 八 分 分						

164

然	然	然	rán: (然后 : then, afterwards) 然后	huǒ 火 (灬) fire					
				然 然					
ノ	ク	タ	夕	夕一	夘	夕犬	狄	狄	狄	然	然

165

图	图	圖	tú: picture (图书馆 : library) 图书馆	wéi 囗 enclosure					
				图 图					
丨	冂	冂	冈	図	図	图	图		

馆	馆	館	guǎn: house, hall 图书馆	shí 食 (饣) food					
				馆 馆					
ノ	𠂉	饣	饣	饣	饣	馆	馆	馆	馆	馆

午	午	午	wǔ: noon 下午	piě ノ left slanted stroke					
				午 午					
ノ	𠂉	午	午						

喜	喜	喜	xǐ: happy; like 喜欢	kǒu 口 mouth					
				喜 喜					
一	十	士	吉	吉	亭	喜	喜		

欢	欢	歡	huān: joyfully (喜欢 : like) 喜欢	qiàn 欠 owe					
				欢 欢					
フ	又	又	欢	欢	欢				

170	球	球 球	qiú: ball 打球	yù 玉(王) jade 球 球		
		一 二 于 王 王一 玎 玎 玎 球 球 球				

171	写	写 寫	xiě: write 写信	mì ⌐ cover 写 写		
		′ 宀 勹 写 写				

172	信	信 信	xìn: letter 写信	rén 人(亻) person 信 信		
		亻 信 信 信				

173	子	子 子	zǐ: (电子: electron) 电子	zǐ 子 child 子 子		
		⌐ 了 子				

174	邮	邮 郵	yóu: mail 邮件	yì 邑(阝) city 邮 邮		
		丨 口 曰 由 由 由了 邮				

175	件	件 件	jiàn: letter (邮件: mail) 邮件	rén 人(亻) person 件 件		
		ノ 亻 亻 仁 仵 件				

| 地 | 地 地 | dì: land
地址 | tǔ 土
earth
地 地 | | | | |
| | 一 十 土 地 | | | | | | |

| 址 | 址 址 | zhǐ: location
地址 | tǔ 土
earth
址 址 | | | | |
| | 土 圵 圤 址 址 | | | | | | |

| 祝 | 祝 祝 | zhù: wish | shì 示 (礻)
reveal
祝 祝 | | | | |
| | 礻 礻刀 礻刃 祝 | | | | | | |

| 年 | 年 年 | nián: year
二〇〇三年 | piě 丿
left slanted
stroke
年 年 | | | | |
| | 丿 𠂉 乍 午 𠂤 年 | | | | | | |

| 月 | 月 月 | yuè: month
十一月 | ròu 肉 (月)
meat
月 月 | | | | |
| | 丿 刀 月 月 | | | | | | |

| 日 | 日 日 | rì: day
二十日 | rì 日
sun
日 日 | | | | |
| | 丨 冂 𠃌 日 | | | | | | |

第十课 ▪ 我每天七点半起床 **Lesson 10** ▪ *I Get Up at 7:30 Every Day* **143**

Lesson 11   Do You Want Black Tea or Green Tea?

红	红	红	hóng: red 红茶	mì 糸 (纟) silk			
				红 红			
	纟	纟	纟	纟	红	红	

茶	茶	茶	chá: tea 喝茶	cǎo 艸 (艹) grass			
				茶 茶			
	艹	艾	苃	苶	荼	茶	

还	还	還	hái: (还是: or) 还是	chuò 辵 (辶) motion			
				还 还			
	一	丆	不	不	不	还	还

绿	绿	綠	lǜ: green 绿茶	mì 糸 (纟) silk			
				绿 绿			
	纟	纟	纟	纠	纪	纪	纾	纾	纾	绿	绿

服	服	服	fú: serve 服务员	ròu 肉 (月) meat			
				服 服			
	月	朋	朋	那	服		

务 (187)	务 務	wù: be engaged in 服务员	lì 力 strength 务 务
员 (188)	员 員	yuán: person 服务员	kǒu 口 mouth 员 员
坐 (189)	坐 坐	zuò: sit 请坐	tǔ 土 earth 坐 坐
先 (190)	先 先	xiān: (先生: sir, Mr.) 先生	ér 儿 walking man 先 先
喝 (191)	喝 喝	hē: drink 喝茶	kǒu 口 mouth 喝 喝
杯 (192)	杯 杯	bēi: cup 一杯红茶	mù 木 wood 杯 杯

Stroke orders:
- 务: ノ ク 夂 冬 务
- 员: 丶 丨 冂 口 尸 呂 员 员
- 坐: ノ 人 𠆢 从 丛 坐 坐
- 先: ノ 𠂉 牛 生 牛 先
- 喝: 口 叩 叩 吅 咽 咽 喝 喝 喝 喝
- 杯: 木 杯

冰	冰 冰	bīng: ice 冰红茶	bīng 冫 ice	冰 冰			
	、 丶 冫 冴 冰 冰						

乐	乐 樂	lè: happy (可乐: Coke) 可乐	piě 丿 left slanted stroke	乐 乐			
	丿 ⺊ 乐 乐 乐						

瓶	瓶 瓶	píng: bottle 一瓶	wǎ 瓦 tile	瓶 瓶			
	丶 丷 ⺷ 兰 羊 并 并 瓶 瓶 瓶						

啤	啤 啤	pí: (啤酒: beer) 啤酒	kǒu 口 mouth	啤 啤			
	口 口′ 口̍ 吅 吅 咱 啤 啤 啤						

酒	酒 酒	jiǔ: liquor, wine, alcoholic drink 啤酒	shuǐ 水 (氵) water	酒 酒			
	氵 氵 沂 沂 沔 酒 酒 酒						

面	面 麵	miàn: noodle 炒面	yī 一 one	面 面			
	一 丆 丆 丙 而 而 面 面						

199	饺	饺	餃	jiǎo: dumpling 饺子	shí 食 (饣) food	饺 饺			
	ノ	𠂇	饣	饣	饣	饣	饣	饺	饺

200	盘	盘	盤	pán: plate, dish 一盘	mǐn 皿 vessel	盘 盘			
	ノ	ノ	刀	舟	舟	舟	舟	舟	盘

01	炒	炒	炒	chǎo: fry 炒饭	huǒ 火 (灬) fire	炒 炒			
	丶	丶	丷	火	灯	灯	炒	炒	

02	十	十	十	shí: ten 十个饺子	shí 十 ten	十 十			
	一	十							

03	碗	碗	碗	wǎn: bowl 一碗饭	shí 石 stone	碗 碗			
	一	丆	丆	石	石	矿	矿	碎	碗

04	汤	汤	湯	tāng: soup 一碗汤	shuǐ 水 (氵) water	汤 汤			
	丶	丶	氵	氵	汤	汤			

| 双 | 双 雙 | shuāng: (M.W.)
一双筷子 | yòu 又
right hand | | |
| | ㄱ 又 刃 双 | | 双 双 | | |

| 筷 | 筷 筷 | kuài: chopsticks
筷子 | zhú 竹 (⺮)
bamboo | | |
| | 竹 筇 筇 筷 筷 筷 | | 筷 筷 | | |

第十一课 ▪ 你要红茶还是绿茶？　**Lesson 11** ▪ *Do You Want Black Tea or Green Tea?*

写字簿生词索引 CHARACTER BOOK INDEX
(BY NUMBER OF STROKES)

Each entry lists simplified character, traditional character, Pinyin, English meaning, and lesson number.

1

一		yī	one	3

2

人		rén	person	3
了		le	Part.	3
儿	兒	ér	(retroflex ending)	3
几	幾	jǐ	how many	5
二		èr	two	7
七		qī	seven	7
八		bā	eight	7
九		jiǔ	nine	7
十		shí	ten	11

3

也		yě	also	1
么	麼	me	什么: what	2
工		gōng	work	4
下		xià	down, get off	5
个	個	gè	M.W.	5
大		dà	big	6
小		xiǎo	small	7
三		sān	three	7
上		shàng	get on, go to	8
门	門	mén	M.W.	10
才		cái	not until	10
子		zǐ	son	10
飞	飛	fēi	fly	12
习	習	xí	practice	12
久		jiǔ	long time	17
女		nǚ	female	20
马	馬	mǎ	horse	20
已		yǐ	already	22

4

不		bù	no, not	1
文		wén	language	2
中		zhōng	middle	2
什		shén	什么: what	2
书	書	shū	book	4
太		tài	too	4
少		shǎo	few, little	4
从	從	cóng	from	5
友		yǒu	friend	5
介		jiè	介绍: introduce	5
车	車	chē	vehicle	6
五		wǔ	five	7
六		liù	six	7
手		shǒu	hand	7
认	認	rèn	recognize	8
以		yǐ	以后: after, later	8
今		jīn	today	8
天		tiān	day	8
见	見	jiàn	see	8
分		fēn	minute	10
午		wǔ	noon	10
月		yuè	moon, month	10
日		rì	sun, day	10
双	雙	shuāng	M.W.	11
开	開	kāi	drive	12
比		bǐ	than	13
为	為	wèi	for	14
气	氣	qì	air	14
公		gōng	public	15
厅	廳	tīng	hall	15
氏		shì	华氏: Fahrenheit	17
风	風	fēng	wind	17
火		huǒ	fire	18

方		fāng	square	22
心		xīn	heart	22

处	處	chù	place	22
东	東	dōng	east	22

5

生		shēng	man	1
他		tā	he	1
叫		jiào	call	2
对	對	duì	correct	3
本		běn	M.W.	4
可		kě	but	4
功		gōng	功课: homework	4
们	們	mén	(suffix)	4
四		sì	four	6
只	隻	zhī	M.W.	6
号	號	hào	number	7
电	電	diàn	electricity	7
外		wài	outside	7
去		qù	go	8
正		zhèng	in the process of	9
打		dǎ	strike, beat	9
半		bàn	half	10
写	寫	xiě	write	10
务	務	wù	be engaged in	11
乐	樂	lè	happy	11
用		yòng	use	12
白		bái	white	12
让	讓	ràng	let	13
加		jiā	add	14
边	邊	biān	side	15
业	業	yè	course of study	16
包		bāo	wrap	16
冬		dōng	winter	17
只		zhǐ	only	18
头	頭	tóu	head	19
发	發	fā	feel, send out	19
记	記	jì	record, notes	19
出		chū	out	20
必		bì	must, have to	20
付		fù	pay	20
申		shěn	state, express	21
司		sī	department	21
平		píng	calm, peaceful	21
市		shì	city	22

6

好		hǎo	good, fine	1
生		shēng	student	1
吗	嗎	ma	Part.	1
我		wǒ	I, me	1
老		lǎo	old	1
师	師	shī	teacher	1
问	問	wèn	ask	2
名		míng	name	2
字		zì	character, word	2
她		tā	she, her	2
同		tóng	same	2
会	會	huì	can	3
那		nà	that	4
多		duō	many, much	4
有		yǒu	have	5
在		zài	at, in	6
妈	媽	mā	mother	6
机	機	jī	machine	7
后	後	hòu	later, after	8
回		huí	return	8
吃		chī	eat	8
次		cì	order, sequence	8
行		xíng	okay	8
再		zài	again	8
吧		ba	Part.	9
忙		máng	busy	9
网	網	wǎng	net	9
欢	歡	huān	joyfully	10
件		jiàn	M.W.	10
地		dì	land	10
年		nián	year	10
红	紅	hóng	red	11
先		xiān	先生: sir, Mr.	11
冰		bīng	ice	11
汤	湯	tāng	soup	11
场	場	chǎng	field, spot	12
色		sè	color	12
买	買	mǎi	buy	13
岁	歲	suì	year of age	14

	guò	pass, spend	14
過	guān	observe, look	15
觀	chí	pool	16
華	huá	华氏: Fahrenheit	17
	bǎi	hundred	17
	zì	self	18
	gòng	common	18
	xī	west	18
	kǎo	give or take a test	19
	xiū	休息: rest	19
	xī	inhale	20
關	guān	关系: relation	20
畢	bì	finish	21
決	jué	decide	21
	ān	safe	21
	yīn	because	22
動	dòng	move	22
興	rú	be like, as if	22
	xìng	pleasure	22
	shōu	receive	22

	nǐ	you	1
這	zhè	this	4
來	lái	come	5
兩	liǎng	two	5
	zuò	工作: work	6
	nán	male	6
沒	méi	do not have	6
	zhù	live	7
間	jiān	room	7
識	shí	know, recognize	8
飯	fàn	rice, meal	8
	wèi	M.W.	9
	ba	Part.	9
	yán	speech, words	9
時	shí	time	9
	měi	each, every	10
	chuáng	bed	10
郵	yóu	mail	10
	zhǐ	location	10
還	hái	还是: or	11
員	yuán	person	11

	zuò	sit	11
應	yīng	should	12
進	jìn	enter	12
條	bù	step	12
	tiáo	M.W.	13
	huò	or	13
塊	kuài	M.W.	13
裡	yíng	welcome	15
園	lǐ	inside	15
	zǒu	walk	15
	yuán	garden	15
體	kuài	fast	16
	tǐ	body	16
極	shēn	body	16
	jí	extremely	17
	lěng	cold	17
遠	yuǎn	far	18
	qì	steam, vapor	18
	jìn	near	18
聽	tīng	to listen	18
醫	yī	medical science	19
	bǎ	Prep.	20
係	xì	relate to	20
	dàn	but	20
	jiū	study carefully	21
	zhǎo	look for	21
運	yùn	luck	21
麗	lì	beautiful	22

8

	xué	study, learn	1
學	ne	Part.	1
	xìng	family name	2
	de	Part.	2
	yīng	英文: English	2
國	guó	country	3
	fǎ	法国: France	3
	hé	and	3
	péng	friend	5
紹	shào	介绍: introduce	5
	bà	father	6
	jiě	older sister	6
	gǒu	dog	6

思		sī	think, consider	21
城		chéng	city, town	22
尝	嚐	cháng	taste	22
保		bǎo	protect, maintain	22
重		zhòng	heavy	22
笔	筆	bǐ	pen	19
啊		ā	an exclamation	20
烟	煙	yān	smoke	20
脑	腦	nǎo	brain	21
班		bān	class	21
告		gào	to tell	22
剧	劇	jù	opera, play	22

10

请	請	qǐng	please	2
谁	誰	shuí	who	2
难	難	nán	difficult	4
课	課	kè	class	4
都		dōu	all	5
家		jiā	home, family	6
爱	愛	ài	love	6
校		xiào	school	7
起		qǐ	一起: together	8
样	樣	yàng	appearance	8
留		liú	leave, remain	9
候		hòu	time	9
球		qiú	ball	10
瓶		píng	bottle	11
酒		jiǔ	wine	11
借		jiè	borrow	12
能		néng	can, may	12
较	較	jiào	compare	13
钱	錢	qián	money	13
旁		páng	side	15
桌		zhuō	table	15
真		zhēn	really, truly	15
健		jiàn	healthy	16
夏		xià	summer	17
热	熱	rè	hot	17
旅		lǚ	travel	18
离	離	lí	leave, away from	18
骑	騎	qí	ride	18
部		bù	part	18
海		hǎi	sea	18
租		zū	rent	18
饿	餓	è	hungry	19
疼		téng	ache, pain	19
烧	燒	shāo	burn	19
病		bìng	be sick	19
息		xī	rest	19
准	準	zhǔn	accurate	19

11

您		nín	you (polite way)	2
常		cháng	often	5
辆	輛	liàng	M.W.	6
宿		sù	stay overnight	7
菜		cài	dish	8
做		zuò	do	9
晚		wǎn	late	9
馆	館	guǎn	house, hall	10
绿	綠	lǜ	green	11
啤		pí	啤酒: beer	11
盘	盤	pán	plate, dish	11
得		děi	have to	12
接		jiē	receive, pick up	12
排		pái	排挡: gear	12
停		tíng	stop, park	12
黄	黃	huáng	yellow	13
张	張	zhāng	M.W.	13
票		piào	ticket	13
蛋		dàn	egg	14
教		jiào/jiāo	teach	16
假		jià	vacation, holiday	17
雪		xuě	snow	17
船		chuán	ship, boat	18
第		dì	(prefix)	20
笼	籠	lóng	cage, steamer	22

12

程		chéng	工程: engineering	4
喂		wèi/wéi	hello	9
等		děng	wait	9
道		dào	road, talk	9
谢	謝	xiè	thank	9
就		jiù	Adv.	9
期		qī	period	10

Each entry lists simplified character, traditional character, Pinyin, and English meaning.

Lesson 1

你 | | nǐ | you
好 | | hǎo | good
是 | | shì | is, are
学 | 學 | xué | study
生 | | shēng | student
吗 | 嗎 | ma | Part.
我 | | wǒ | I, me
呢 | | ne | Part.
也 | | yě | also, too
他 | | tā | he, him
不 | | bù | not
老 | | lǎo | old
师 | 師 | shī | teacher

Lesson 2

您 | | nín | (polite) you
贵 | 貴 | guì | noble, honored
姓 | | xìng | family name
请 | 請 | qǐng | please
问 | 問 | wèn | ask
的 | | de | Part.
英 | | yīng | 英文: English
文 | | wén | language, writing
名 | | míng | name
字 | | zì | character, word
中 | | zhōng | middle
叫 | | jiào | call
什 | | shén | 什么: what
么 | 麼 | me | 什么: what
她 | | tā | she, her
谁 | 誰 | shéi | who, whom
同 | | tóng | same, similar

Lesson 3

哪 | | nǎ | which
国 | 國 | guó | country
人 | | rén | person
很 | | hěn | very
对 | 對 | duì | correct
了 | | le | Part.
法 | | fǎ | 法国: France
美 | | měi | beautiful
说 | 說 | shuō | speak
会 | 會 | huì | be able to
一 | | yī | one
点 | 點 | diǎn | dot
儿 | 兒 | ér | (retroflex ending)
和 | | hé | and

Lesson 4

那 | | nà | that
书 | 書 | shū | book
这 | 這 | zhè | this
本 | | běn | M.W.
工 | | gōng | work
程 | | chéng | 工程: engineering
难 | 難 | nán | difficult
太 | | tài | too
可 | | kě | but
功 | | gōng | 功课: homework
课 | 課 | kè | class
多 | | duō | many, much
们 | 們 | men | (suffix)
少 | | shǎo | few, little

Lesson 5

朋		péng	friend
友		yǒu	friend
来	來	lái	come
介		jiè	介绍: introduce
绍	紹	shào	介绍: introduce
下		xià	down; get off
室		shì	room
有		yǒu	have
几	幾	jǐ	how many
两	兩	liǎng	two
个	個	gè	M.W.
都		dōu	all; both
常		cháng	often
跟		gēn	with

Lesson 6

家		jiā	home
大		dà	big
从	從	cóng	from
在		zài	at, in
四		sì	four
爸		bà	dad
妈	媽	mā	mom
姐		jiě	older sister
作		zuò	工作: work
男		nán	male
没	沒	méi	don't have
辆	輛	liàng	M.W. for vehicles
车	車	chē	car
只	隻	zhī	M.W.
狗		gǒu	dog
爱	愛	ài	love

Lesson 7

住		zhù	live
宿		sù	stay overnight
舍		shè	house
号	號	hào	number
房		fáng	house
间	間	jiān	room
电	電	diàn	electricity

(Lesson 7 continued)

话	話	huà	word
小		xiǎo	small
码	碼	mǎ	number
二		èr	two
三		sān	three
五		wǔ	five
六		liù	six
七		qī	seven
八		bā	eight
九		jiǔ	nine
手		shǒu	hand
机	機	jī	machine
校		xiào	school
外		wài	outside

Lesson 8

认	認	rèn	know, recognize
识	識	shí	know, recognize
去		qù	go
上		shàng	get on, attend
以		yǐ	以后: after, later
后	後	hòu	behind
事		shì	matter, thing
想		xiǎng	want, think
回		huí	return
起		qǐ	一起: together
吃		chī	eat
饭	飯	fàn	rice, meal
菜		cài	dish
今		jīn	today
天		tiān	day
次		cì	order, sequence
怎		zěn	how
样	樣	yàng	appearance
行		xíng	okay
再		zài	again
见	見	jiàn	see

Lesson 9

打		dǎ	hit, play, make
喂		wèi/wéi	hello, hey
等		děng	wait

知		zhī	know
道		dào	road, walk
谢	謝	xiè	thanks
吧		ba	Part.
忙		máng	busy
正		zhèng	in process of
看		kàn	see, watch
视	視	shì	look
做		zuò	do
网	網	wǎng	net
就		jiù	Adv.
位		wèi	M.W.
留		liú	leave, remain
言		yán	speech, words
时	時	shí	time
候		hòu	time
晚		wǎn	night, late
要		yào	want
给	給	gěi	give; for, to

Lesson 10

活		huó	live
期		qī	a period of time
门	門	mén	M.W.
每		měi	every, each
床		chuáng	bed
睡		shuì	sleep
觉	覺	jiào	sleep
半		bàn	half
才		cái	Adv.
刻		kè	a quarter
分		fēn	minute
然		rán	然后: then
图	圖	tú	picture
馆	館	guǎn	house, hall
午		wǔ	noon
喜		xǐ	happy; like
欢	歡	huān	joyfully
球		qiú	ball
写	寫	xiě	write
信		xìn	letter
子		zǐ	(suffix)
邮	郵	yóu	mail

件		jiàn	letter
地		dì	land
址		zhǐ	location
祝		zhù	wish
年		nián	year
月		yuè	month
日		rì	day

Lesson 11

红	紅	hóng	red
茶		chá	tea
还	還	hái	还是: or
绿	綠	lǜ	green
服		fú	serve
务	務	wù	be engaged in
员	員	yuán	person
坐		zuò	sit
先		xiān	先生: sir, Mr.
喝		hē	drink
杯		bēi	cup
冰		bīng	ice
乐	樂	lè	happy
瓶		píng	bottle
啤		pí	beer
酒		jiǔ	liquor
面	麵	miàn	noodle
饺	餃	jiǎo	dumpling
盘	盤	pán	plate
炒		chǎo	fry
十		shí	ten
碗		wǎn	bowl
汤	湯	tāng	soup
双	雙	shuāng	pair
筷		kuài	chopsticks

Lesson 12

借		jiè	borrow
明		míng	tomorrow
用		yòng	use
得		děi	have to
场	場	chǎng	site
接		jiē	receive

妹 飞 玩 到 排 挡 开 应 该 题 白 色 停 习 练 能 进 步

		mèi	younger sister
飛		fēi	fly
		wán	play
		dào	arrive
		pái	line
擋		dǎng	gear
開 應		kāi	drive
該		yīng	should
題		gāi	should
		tí	problem, topic
		bái	white
		sè	color
		tíng	stop, park
習		xí	practice
練		liàn	practice
		néng	can, may
進		jìn	move forward
		bù	step

Lesson 13

买 衬 衫 店 条 裙 或 者 裤 黄 错 比 较 穿 黑 试 帮 让 钱 块 张 影 票

		mǎi	buy
買 襯		chèn	襯衫: shirt
		shān	shirt, clothes
		diàn	shop
條		tiáo	M.W.
		qún	skirt
		huò	or
		zhě	或者: or
褲 黃 錯		kù	pants
		huáng	yellow
		cuò	wrong
		bǐ	compare
較		jiào	compare
		chuān	wear
		hēi	black
試 幫 讓 錢 塊 張		shì	try
		bāng	help
		ràng	let
		qián	money
		kuài	dollar
		zhāng	M.W.
		yǐng	shadow, movie
		piào	ticket

Lesson 14

岁 空 星 过 为 舞 参 加 定 蛋 糕 送 棒 客 气

歲		suì	year (of age)
		kòng	free time
		xīng	star
過 為 參		guò	spend
		wèi	for
		wǔ	dance
		cān	join
		jiā	add
		dìng	surely
		dàn	egg
		gāo	cake
		sòng	give as a present
		bàng	good, excellent
		kè	guest
氣		qì	air

Lesson 15

前 边 迎 观 里 厨 公 旁 走 厅 面 餐 洗 澡 卧 桌 园 真

		qián	front
邊		biān	side
觀 裡 廚		yíng	greet
		guān	observe
		lǐ	inside
		chú	kitchen
		gōng	public
		páng	side
		zǒu	walk
廳		tīng	hall
		miàn	surface
		cān	meal, food
		xǐ	wash
		zǎo	bath
臥		wò	lie
		zhuō	table
園		yuán	a piece of land
		zhēn	really

Lesson 16

篮 俩 教

籃 俩		lán	basket
		liǎ	two
		jiào/jiāo	teach

游		yóu	swim
泳		yǒng	swim
非		fēi	wrong, not
快		kuài	fast
体	體	tǐ	body
育		yù	educate
池		chí	pool
健		jiàn	healthy
身		shēn	body
锻	鍛	duàn	forge
炼	煉	liàn	refine
现	現	xiàn	now
昨		zuó	yesterday
赛	賽	sài	game, match
业	業	yè	course of study
包		bāo	wrap
慢		màn	slow

Lesson 17

春		chūn	spring
久		jiǔ	long
放		fàng	put, release
假		jià	vacation
夏		xià	summer
秋		qiū	fall, autumn
冬		dōng	winter
其		qí	that, such
最		zuì	most
暖		nuǎn	warm
短		duǎn	short
热	熱	rè	hot
华	華	huá	华氏: Fahrenheit
氏		shì	华氏: Fahrenheit
百		bǎi	hundred
度		dù	degree
极	極	jí	extreme
刮		guā	blow
风	風	fēng	wind
雨		yǔ	rain
冷		lěng	cold
雪		xuě	snow

Lesson 18

火		huǒ	fire
旅		lǚ	travel
离	離	lí	leave, part from
远	遠	yuǎn	far
只		zhǐ	only
钟	鐘	zhōng	clock
骑	騎	qí	ride
自		zì	self
共		gòng	common
汽		qì	steam
路		lù	road
近		jìn	close
西		xī	west
部		bù	part
景		jǐng	view, scenery
船		chuán	boat, ship
南		nán	south
听	聽	tīng	listen
海		hǎi	sea
租		zū	rent

Lesson 19

感		gǎn	feel, sense
冒		mào	emit, give off
饿	餓	è	hungry
像		xiàng	be like; seem
舒		shū	loosen, relax
头	頭	tóu	head
疼		téng	ache, pain
发	發	fā	feel, send out
烧	燒	shāo	fever
咳		ké	cough
嗽		sòu	cough
病		bìng	sick
考		kǎo	give or take a test
复	復	fù	repeat
所		suǒ	所以: therefore
医	醫	yī	medical science
药	藥	yào	medicine
休		xiū	休息: rest

息		xī	rest
准	準	zhǔn	prepare
备	備	bèi	prepare
笔	筆	bǐ	pen
记	記	jì	notes

Lesson 20

把		bǎ	Prep.
带	帶	dài	bring
啊		a	Int.
搬		bān	move
出		chū	out
吸		xī	inhale
烟	煙	yān	smoke
关	關	guān	concern
系	係	xì	relate to
但		dàn	but
女		nǚ	female
必		bì	must
须	須	xū	must
第		dì	(prefix)
付		fù	pay
楼	樓	lóu	floor
马	馬	mǎ	horse

Lesson 21

暑		shǔ	heat, hot
毕	畢	bì	finish
决	決	jué	decide
申		shēn	express
研		yán	study
究		jiū	study
院		yuàn	institute
找		zhǎo	look for
司		sī	department

实	實	shí	solid
脑	腦	nǎo	brain
班		bān	class
意		yì	meaning
思		sī	think
愉		yú	happy
平		píng	calm, peaceful
安		ān	safe
运	運	yùn	luck

Lesson 22

因		yīn	because
已		yǐ	already
经	經	jīng	pass
丽	麗	lì	beautiful
城		chéng	city
市		shì	city
处	處	chù	place
新		xīn	new
些		xiē	some
方		fāng	side, direction
动	動	dòng	move
如		rú	be like
京		jīng	capital
剧	劇	jù	opera, drama
东	東	dōng	east
笼	籠	lóng	cage, steamer
尝	嚐	cháng	taste
始		shǐ	beginning
高		gāo	high
兴	興	xìng	pleasure
收		shōu	receive
心		xīn	heart
板		bǎn	老板: boss
保		bǎo	protect, maintain
重		zhòng	heavy

写字簿生词索引　CHARACTER BOOK INDEX
(ALPHABETICAL BY PINYIN)

Each entry lists simplified character, traditional character, Pinyin, English meaning, and lesson number.

A

啊		a	Int.	20
爱	愛	ài	love	6
安		ān	safe	21

B

吧		ba	Part.	9
八		bā	eight	7
把		bǎ	Prep.	20
爸		bà	dad	6
白		bái	white	12
百		bǎi	hundred	17
搬		bān	move	20
班		bān	class	21
板	闆	bǎn	老板: boss	22
半		bàn	half	10
帮	幫	bāng	help	13
棒		bàng	good, excellent	14
包		bāo	wrap	16
保		bǎo	maintain	22
杯		bēi	cup	11
备	備	bèi	prepare	19
本		běn	M.W.	4
比		bǐ	compare	13
笔	筆	bǐ	pen	19
必		bì	must, have to	20
毕	畢	bì	finish	21
边	邊	biān	side	15
冰		bīng	ice	11
病		bìng	be sick; disease	19
不		bù	no, not	1
步		bù	step, pace	12
部		bù	part	18

C

才		cái	Adv.	10
菜		cài	dish	8
参	參	cān	join	14
餐		cān	meal	15
茶		chá	tea	11
常		cháng	often	5
尝	嘗	cháng	taste	22
场	場	chǎng	site, spot	12
炒		chǎo	fry	11
车	車	chē	car	6
衬	襯	chèn	衬衫: shirt	13
程		chéng	工程: engineering	4
城		chéng	city	22
吃		chī	eat	8
池		chí	pool	16
出		chū	out	20
厨	廚	chú	kitchen	15
处	處	chù	place	22
穿		chuān	wear	13
船		chuán	boat, ship	18
床		chuáng	bed	10
春		chūn	spring	17
次		cì	order, sequence	8
从	從	cóng	from	6
错	錯	cuò	wrong	13

D

打		dǎ	hit, play	9
大		dà	big	6
带	帶	dài	bring	20
蛋		dàn	egg	14
但		dàn	but	20

机	機	jī	machine	7
极	極	jí	extreme	17
几	幾	jǐ	how many	5
记	記	jì	note, record	19
家		jiā	home	6
加		jiā	add	14
假		jià	holiday	17
间	間	jiān	room	7
见	見	jiàn	see	8
件		jiàn	邮件: letter	10
健		jiàn	healthy	16
教		jiāo	teach	16
饺	餃	jiǎo	dumpling	11
叫		jiào	call	2
觉	覺	jiào	sleep	10
较	較	jiào	compare	13
教		jiào	教练: coach	16
接		jiē	receive	12
姐		jiě	older sister	6
介		jiè	介绍: introduce	5
借		jiè	borrow, lend	12
今		jīn	now, this	8
进	進	jìn	move forward	12
近		jìn	near, close	18
经	經	jīng	pass	22
京		jīng	capital	22
景		jǐng	view, scenery	18
究		jiū	study carefully	21
九		jiǔ	nine	7
酒		jiǔ	liquor	11
久		jiǔ	long	17
就		jiù	Adv.	9
剧	劇	jù	opera, play	22
决	決	jué	decide	21
觉	覺	jué	feel	10

K

开	開	kāi	drive, open	12
看		kàn	see, watch	9
考		kǎo	give or take a test	19
咳		ké	cough	19
可		kě	but	4

课	課	kè	class	4
刻		kè	a quarter	10
客		kè	guest, visit	14
空		kòng	free time	14
裤	褲	kù	pants	13
筷		kuài	chopsticks	11
块	塊	kuài	dollar, piece	13
快		kuài	fast	16

L

来	來	lái	come	5
篮	籃	lán	basket	16
老		lǎo	老师: teacher	1
了		le	Part.	3
乐	樂	lè	happy	11
冷		lěng	cold	17
离	離	lí	leave, away	18
里		lǐ	inside	15
丽	麗	lì	beautiful	22
俩	倆	liǎ	two	16
练	練	liàn	practice	12
炼	煉	liàn	refine	16
两	兩	liǎng	two	5
辆	輛	liàng	M.W.	6
留		liú	leave	9
六		liù	six	7
笼	籠	lóng	cage	22
楼	樓	lóu	floor	20
路		lù	road	18
旅		lǚ	travel	18
绿	綠	lǜ	green	11

M

吗	嗎	ma	Part.	1
妈	媽	mā	mom	6
码	碼	mǎ	code	7
马	馬	mǎ	horse	20
买	買	mǎi	buy	13
慢		màn	slow	16
忙		máng	busy	9
冒		mào	emit, give off	19
么	麼	me	什么: what	2

没	沒	méi	no	6
美		měi	美国: USA	3
每		měi	every	10
妹		mèi	younger sister	12
们	們	men	(suffix)	4
门	門	mén	M.W.	10
面	麵	miàn	noodle	11
面		miàn	surface	15
名		míng	name	2
明		míng	bright, tomorrow	12

N

哪		nǎ	which	3
那		nà	that	4
难	難	nán	difficult	4
男		nán	male	6
南		nán	south	18
脑	腦	nǎo	brain	21
呢		ne	Part.	1
能		néng	can, may	12
你		nǐ	you	1
年		nián	year	10
您		nín	(polite) you	2
暖		nuǎn	warm	17
女		nǚ	female	20

P

排		pái	排挡: gear	12
盘	盤	pán	dish	11
旁		páng	side	15
朋		péng	朋友: friend	5
啤		pí	啤酒: beer	11
票		piào	ticket	13
瓶		píng	bottle	11
平		píng	peace	21

Q

七		qī	seven	7
期		qī	a period of time	10
其		qí	其中: among	17
骑	騎	qí	ride	18
起		qǐ	一起: together	8

气	氣	qì	air	14
汽		qì	vapor	18
钱	錢	qián	money	13
前		qián	front	15
请	請	qǐng	please	2
秋		qiū	autumn	17
球		qiú	ball	10
去		qù	go	8
裙		qún	skirt	13

R

然		rán	然后: then	10
让	讓	ràng	let	13
热	熱	rè	hot	17
人		rén	person	3
认	認	rèn	认识: know	8
日		rì	day	10
如		rú	be like, as if	22

S

赛	賽	sài	game, match	16
三		sān	three	7
色		sè	color	12
衫		shān	shirt	13
上		shàng	on, go to	8
烧	燒	shāo	fever	19
少		shǎo	few, little	4
绍	紹	shào	介绍: introduce	5
舍		shè	house, shed	7
谁	誰	shéi	who	2
身		shēn	body	16
申		shēn	state, express	21
什		shén	什么: what	2
生		shēng	学生: student	1
师	師	shī	老师: teacher	1
识	識	shí	know, recognize	8
时	時	shí	time	9
十		shí	ten	11
实	實	shí	实习: intern	21
始		shǐ	beginning	22
是		shì	to be, yes	1
室		shì	room	5
事		shì	matter, thing	8

Y

Z

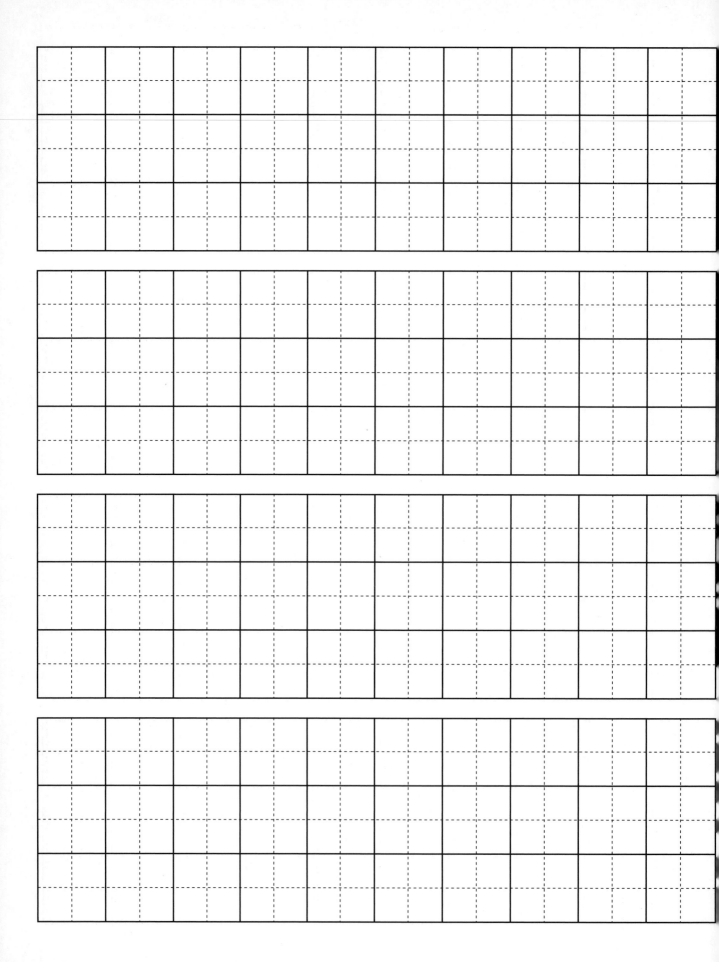